This is Christianity

Ashley Choudhry

This is Christianity
for Students

Peter Cotterell

This book is produced for student-run Christian Unions to explain how living Christianity relates to contemporary society.

Christian Unions are not scalp hunting but would be very glad to hear from anyone who is concerned to find the answers to life's most important questions. Your local group will give more information or write to Ken Wycherley at the UCCF address overleaf.

INTER-VARSITY PRESS

Inter-Varsity Press
38 De Montfort Street, Leicester LE1 7GP, England
© Peter Cotterell 1985

Unless otherwise stated, quotations from the Bible are
taken from the HOLY BIBLE: NEW INTERNATIONAL
VERSION, © 1978 by the International Bible Society,
New York. Published in Great Britain by Hodder and
Stoughton Ltd., and used by permission of Zondervan
Bible Publishers, Grand Rapids, Michigan

First published 1985

ISBN 0-85110-478-9

Typeset in Melior by
Parker Typesetting Service, Leicester

Printed and bound in Great Britain by
Richard Clay (The Chaucer Press) Ltd,
Bungay, Suffolk

Inter-Varsity Press is the publishing division of the
Universities and Colleges Christian Fellowship
(formerly the Inter-Varsity Fellowship), a student
movement linking Christian Unions in universities and
colleges throughout the United Kingdom and the Republic
of Ireland, and a member movement of the International
Fellowship of Evangelical Students. For information
about local and national activities write to UCCF, 38
De Montfort Street, Leicester LE1 7GP.

Contents

1
Basic questions

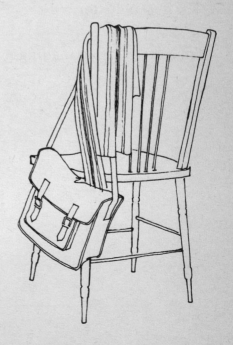

Anne came in from school one day and burst out:

It's not fair!

Well, it wasn't fair. Cheating at school went on all the time. The children passed bits of paper around with the right answers on them. They talked during tests, copied one another's homework, and the girls who did it flourished! No thunderbolts from heaven. No thunderbolts even from the teachers. They seemed to get away with cheating.

It would have been nice to have been able to say to Anne that their dishonesty would catch up with them eventually. But it doesn't always. Some people are able to go right through life lying and cheating and swindling, and it never does catch up with them. On the contrary, they flourish. It's not fair.

And there's the heart-break problem of physical suffering. Just recently a baby was born. I've known the parents ever since *they* were born, even baby-sat one of them while *his* parents had a night off. They'd looked forward to the birth, but their baby was born dreadfully malformed. A few months later it died. But *why*? Why should it happen to them?

There's the glaring unfairness of overflowing riches and abject poverty.

As I was writing this book a cabinet was being sold in London. Something rather special, I gathered. It must have been, because it was sold for more than nine hundred thousand pounds . . . nearly a million. The newspapers said that the buyer had a bargain. But . . . almost a million pounds for a fancy box? I worked it out at three million meals for starving people. In a world where people are starving, buying a box for a fortune doesn't make sense.

At some point in our lives most of us find life perplexing. It doesn't seem to make sense. 'It isn't fair!'

The cry is torn out of us by some of these experiences, illness, accident, death, hunger, war, earthquake . . . so much suffering.

Deep down inside most of us respond in a kind of frustrated anger: 'It isn't fair!' Life doesn't seem to make sense.

This observation suggests one

Caracas: the stark contrast of rich and poor

way of viewing religion: as an attempt to make sense of life. In fact Buddhism has a technical word for this in-built unsatisfactoriness of life: *dukkha*. In Buddhism *dukkha*, 'unsatisfactoriness', is one of the three characteristics of life. Life is:

- *anicca*, impermanent
- *dukkha*, unsatisfactory
- *anatta*, impersonal

Buddhism then goes on to offer an explanation of *why* life is like that and how we might begin to make sense of it.

Now the world's religions disa-

tions, then we will be able to explain *dukkha*, this general unsatisfactoriness of life.

Of course there are various ways of defining 'religion'. Mine isn't the only definition, and it has no particular authority behind it. If we make use of this definition, however, we can include under the label 'religion' all those systems which we would intuitively recognize as religions: Christianity, Islam and Judaism (the three monotheistic religions), Hinduism and Buddhism, Taoism and Confucianism, African Traditional

---

A religion is any system of thinking that offers answers to the basic questions.

There are three series of basic questions:

Who am I? | Who are you?
Where did I come from? | Where did you come from?
Where am I going to? | Where are you going to?
Why? | Why?

What is this world?
Where did it come from?
Where is it going to?
Why?

---

gree about the nature of life and the way in which we might hope to make sense of life, but they all agree on this one thing: life *ought* to make sense. In fact the task of any religion might be seen as that of making sense out of apparent nonsense, the task of explaining *dukkha*, the general unsatisfactoriness of life.

Since I'm going to be saying a good deal about religion I'll need to offer some kind of definition. Scores of definitions have been proposed but I'll be using the one outlined above.

The expectation of the world's religions is that, if we can get sensible answers to the basic ques-

Religion and Sikhism, and other polytheistic and agnostic religions.

Marxism is a little different from the others since it is essentially atheistic. But on my definition it is still a religion because it does offer answers to the basic questions, and it expects its followers to *believe* in those answers. It pictures the ultimate collapse of the world's class system, and the triumph of the proletariat. It is wedded to the theory of evolution, and this would determine Marxism's answer to the question 'Who am I?'. Marxism does not believe that life is meaningless: there is a law to life, the process of inter-action between the present system and its opposite, to produce a new society; thesis, antithesis, synthesis, ultimately leading to a good and just society ... that's where we're going. According to Marxism.

That helps to explain why it is that Marxism is generally in conflict with religions, and particularly in conflict with Christianity. It is itself a religion. As a religion, it can substitute for another religion. Just as in languages you can substitute a verb for a verb because they belong to the same class of words, so Marxism can (and according to Marxists *should*) displace Christianity and

Karl Marx (1818–1883)

other religions because it, too, is a religion. Presumably, for the Marxist, the *best* religion.

Now that we have defined 'religion', and stated the basic questions, we are able to make a vital observation: careful and honest scholarship does not permit us to say that all religions are really the same, essentially saying the same thing. John Kane writes[1]: 'Detailed scholarly work in the history of religions has shown ... facile assertions of unity to be without base'

The fact is that the world's religions do not disagree merely on secondary matters, but also about the central issues. They differ about the answers to the basic questions.

There isn't room in a book of this size to deal with each of the basic questions in detail, but even the superficial survey of the questions and the answers offered by the world's religions makes John Kane's point clear.

Who am I?

Where did I come from?   Where am I going to?   Why?

The first series of questions, most naturally arises out of our own awareness of the two natural terminuses of life: birth and death. Where was I, if anywhere, before I was born? Where will I be, if anywhere, after I die?

Eastern religions such as Buddhism and Hinduism offer openended answers to these questions. You *were* before you were born, and you *will be* after you die. You are caught, trapped in the endless cycle of existence, *samsara*. Unless something happens to break the cycle you will continue indefinitely being born, dying, being

born once more only to die again. The goal of life must be to break out of the cycle, in fact, to put an end to the elusive and delusive 'me'. Buddhism offers *Nirvana* in which all the emotions that are together 'me' are blown out. Hinduism offers absorption into the Absolute. Either pathway means the end of 'me'. C. S. Lewis[2] commented on the commonly used analogy of a drop of water running into the ocean. He put it that if the drop of water runs into the ocean it can be thought of as still existing, but that's the end of it *as a drop*. If I am to be absorbed into the

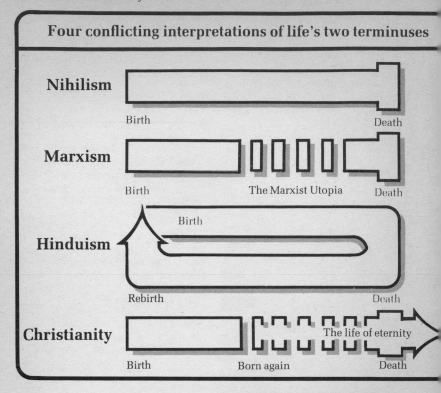

Four conflicting interpretations of life's two terminuses

Nihilism

Birth   Death

Marxism

Birth   The Marxist Utopia   Death

Hinduism

Birth

Rebirth   Death

Christianity

The life of eternity

Birth   Born again   Death

Absolute that's the end of me *as me*.

Christianity responds to this series of questions differently.

I am a unique individual. I was created by God. I had a beginning but I shall not have an ending. Why was I created? In order to enjoy God; to know him, personally.

The answer to the question 'Where am I going?' is complicated by the Christian explanation of *dukkha*, the general unsatisfactoriness of life. For Christians agree that life appears to be unsatisfactory. It is so because we have lost that vital relationship with God, the very thing for which we were created. We have become too clever, too self-confident, arrogant. Foolishly we have come to believe that we

A polluted beach in Wales

- life has no meaning
- there is nothing before birth, nothing after death

- life has meaning: the struggle towards the classless society

- life is an endless cycle of birth and rebirth

- life *should* have meaning and will go on beyond 'death'

can manage the affairs of the world without any reference to God. We abuse our power, our knowledge. We exploit the world, God's world, and ruin it. In Africa the Sahel desert spreads. In Europe the seas become polluted, dumping-places for our atomic waste. Whole species of animals become endangered and then extinct. The Christian explanation of *dukkha* is simple: we have left God out of the equation. Put him back in and all could be different.

Put God back in, and the answer to the question 'Where am I going?' is what it was when man was first made: 'To God, to heaven, to paradise.'

But if not? If I will not allow God to put my life straight, forgiving sin past, freeing me from sin present, what then? Then I shall continue to be part of *dukkha*. I shall be discontented myself and I shall make others discontented.

Note, however, the Christian answer: it can never be I, myself, who by some great effort puts myself right. God must do it. I cannot.

So we ask the question 'Why?'. Why did God bother to create *me*? Even more, having created me, and having seen me turn away from him and go my own way, why did he then come seeking me, instead of simply wiping me off his register? If the world's *dukkha* is simply the sum total of all the godlessness of people like me, why doesn't God simply end us all and start over again somewhere?

The answer is the love of God.

He is *not* a far off, uncaring, remote, gigantic monster. Christianity presents God as a loving Father.

Yet he is *just*, not a sentimental doting grandfather figure who simply overlooks all the naughtiness of the grandchildren. A just God *will* have the books balance: one day. He'll settle the debt, or you will, but it must be settled. Years ago I read of a Canadian farmer who decided to challenge the God of Christianity. He hit on the idea of deliberately working on Sunday, the Christian day of worship. After the September harvest he wrote to his local newspaper: 'I ploughed that field on Sunday, I sowed the grain on Sunday, I reaped it on Sunday and eventually I sold it on Sunday. And I made a greater profit on that field than on any other of my fields.' The editor contented himself with a one-line response: 'God doesn't settle his accounts in September.'

Who are you?

Where did you come from?   Where are you going to?   Why?

The second series of basic questions recognizes that we live in society. There's *me* and there's *you*. Surely it's obvious that my understanding of who *you* are will determine how I treat you. Stalin could exterminate those who opposed him because Marxism believes that the 'you' is unimportant. Kolakowski wrote in *Main Currents of Marxism*[3]: 'Millions were arrested, hundreds of thousands executed'.

Buddhism defines life as impermanent, unsatisfactory and *impersonal*. 'You' do not exist. The individual is an appearance only, an illusion, *maya*. 'You' are a temporary collection of ever-changing constituents, but with no 'you' to hold them together. 'You' do not exist.

Christianity gives a different answer.

You, too, are a unique individual and it is not God's intention to lose or to destroy that individuality.

You are not meant to be 'absorbed' into the Eternal. That body of yours is for ever changing: it grows, strengthens, declines, weakens, eventually disintegrates. But *you* are a uniquely created individual, an unrepeatable combination of what you inherited through the genes which came to you from your parents, what you have learnt and experienced in life, and what God has done for you and in you. You have a unique collection of gifts and abilities, and they are to be found, in that particular combination, only in you. You are irreplaceable. You are valuable to God.

More than that, however, Christianity insists that God has a unique purpose for your life: good, perfect, pleasing (see Romans 12:2). You did not come into existence by accident, the mechanical consequence of a particular sex-act of your parents. The sex-act has occurred millions of times in history without resulting in conception. When it does so Christians see it as an act of God: God gladly giving life. He it was who deliberately brought you into being.

For those of us who appear to be nobodies in this world this is a tremendous thought. I am not unwanted. Possibly my parents did not want me: God does!

So again we have a series of very clear answers to the basic questions:

You, too, are:
- a unique individual
- created by God and moving towards heaven
- living now in a joyful awareness of God
- gladly and humbly related to him

Or
- you are separated from God
- oblivious of him
- not reconciled to him
- part of the world's problem, part of *dukkha*, this unsatisfactoriness of life
- heading not for eternity with God, but for eternity without him

What is this world?

Where did it come from?   Where is it going to?   Why?

Along with Islam and Judaism (but *not* Hinduism and Buddhism) Christianity teaches that God made the world. It had a beginning and it will one day be put aside, finished with. It is not eternal, as Hinduism suggests, nor is it a mere cosmic accident, as Marxism would suggest. The earth was uniquely created by God, intended to be 'home' for us. A little further from our sun and it would be too cold; a little nearer, and it would be too hot. We have the moon so that the nights may be lightened . . . and we spin about the axis so that we have night and day, and all parts of the earth may be warmed . . . oxygen to be breathed . . . an ozone layer to protect man from unacceptable levels of radiation.

But isn't something missing? Life is still unsatisfactory. It's easy enough to argue that some of life's catastrophes are man-made, but not all of them. There's disease, crop failure, pests of all kinds, bacteria. Rabbits are all very well, but what about myxomatosis, the disease that wiped out tens of thousands of them? Where did it come from? If God made the world, he surely made a poor job of it?

A poor job?

Not so, replies the Christian, and offers a double observation on *dukkha*, the unsatisfactoriness of life:

- **This world is not the way it was meant to be.**
- **This world is not the way it is one day going to be.**

What is this world? It is a unique habitat for man. Where did it come from? God made it.

Where is it going? Well, it appears to be out of control. All manner of attempts have been made to put it back on course again. New political systems, local, like African Nationalism, international, like Marxism, are at work attempting to make sense of life, trying to end the unsatisfactory nature of our human existence. These human systems often seem to start with the assumption that we all are basically good, and will be content to work for the good of others and so put the whole world to rights. But the world doesn't go right; the attempt fails. The reason for the unsatisfactory nature of human answers to the question 'Where is

this world going' seems to be found in us. It's not so much the *world* that's the problem as *us*, in the world. The third set of basic questions leads us inexorably back to the first set and the second set.

Where is the world going?

To chaos? Is it God's fault? Well, take the 'unsatisfactoriness' of famine. There's no rain, and the crops fail, so people starve. God's fault? Not so. There is enough food in the world to meet the needs of every-

The wealthy Ethiopians of Addis Ababa had learnt of the plans of the World Bank to develop the area. So they bought up the land from the local people and then sat back and waited for the land to appreciate in value, waited for the right time to sell it to the World Bank. Of course they didn't want to *farm* the land. Meanwhile the thousands starved.

Even that is not the end of the tale. The West learnt of the starvation, sending in milk powder for the children, grain for the hungry.

one alive today and of everyone likely to be alive in the foreseeable future. It's *distribution* that's the problem. It's a mad world when Europe stockpiles its butter and America stockpiles its grain while people in Africa and Asia starve to death, literally, every day.

Wait! It is too easy to blame America and Europe alone. *All* of us – black and white – are to blame for the mess. I lived in Ethiopia for many years, including the famine years, when tens of thousands starved to death. God's fault? America's fault? . . . I flew over the area of southern Ethiopia known locally as the Bread-basket of Africa, mile after mile of marvellously fertile land, but lying fallow.

Ethiopian racketeers got hold of the milk powder and sold it on the open market. As if that didn't give them profit enough, some of them mixed the milk powder with chalk. Babies died, of course. Who is to blame? All of us. The same grasping nature is there in every one of us.

Where is this world going? Our destination is chaos. Often we can't even find a way of helping. Take Ethiopia again. For years there was war on two fronts, with the Somali peoples to the east and with the Eritrean peoples to the north. To back up their demands for maintaining the empire, Ethiopia developed the largest standing army in Africa. Most of the national product went on bombs and bullets. And when in the 1980s famine re-appeared there was a cry for help from the starving thousands. But what was to be done? When grain was sent it encouraged the Ethiopian government to go on squandering its resources on war. And when grain was not sent . . . the people starved.

In addition, of course, there is the horror of disease, earthquake and tornado, all part of the apparent chaos of this world. The world, however, wasn't created like that.

***'God saw all that he had made, and it was very good'* (Genesis 1:31).**

Once again, in Christian teaching, man takes the blame. The third chapter of Genesis simply and dramatically records man's suicidal determination to go it alone, to please himself, to leave God out. In incomparable words we there have spelt out for us the results – man estranged from God, living in a hostile world. In one word: **chaos**.

This chaos is not God's doing, but ours. That's the 'Why?' of the world going into chaos: because of us, and our estrangement from God. If we knew him, we wouldn't and couldn't behave the way we do now.

The cure

Christianity has both an explanation for the chaos, and a cure for it. The explanation we have already seen.

The cure is at two levels:

● immediate
● future

In the short term, God can put a new quality of life, new ambitions, fresh priorities, into us so that we will be prepared to put God first, neighbours second and ourselves last. So, in the short term, we could get a better world. To be realistic we have to say that it would not be the *best* world, simply because Christianity does not encourage us to believe that large numbers of people will walk its way. Christianity is not mere pie-in-the-sky, but the offer of a way, a hard way, starting with us.

At the level of the future, Christianity also has something to say. There is the expectation that one day the world will exhibit all the order, beauty, and purpose that it was originally intended to have. Many of the first Christians were uneducated people. Paul was an exception, a Jew who had studied under a famous teacher, Gamaliel. Paul wrote a letter to the church at Rome and he put the whole picture together very clearly:

All of creation waits with eager longing for God to reveal his sons. For creation was condemned to lose its purpose, not of its own will, but because God willed it to be so. Yet there was the hope that creation itself would

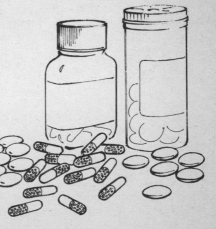

one day be set free from its
slavery to decay and would
share the glorious freedom of the
children of God. For we know
that up to the present time all of
creation groans with pain, like
the pain of childbirth. But it is
not just creation alone which
groans; we who have the Spirit
as the first of God's gifts also
groan within ourselves, as we
wait for God to make us his sons
and set our whole being free
(Romans 8:19–23 GNB).

That is the Christian's long-term
answer to the unsatisfactory
nature of life. God has put me
right, and can put you right.
Between us we can begin to put
this world right. One day, however, God will step in decisively to
set the whole of creation free, so
that we will see God's world as it
was always meant to be.

You will have noticed that again
and again, as we have looked at the
basic questions, we have come
back to ourselves, to people. We do
need to ask ourselves if we are
right in placing man at the very
centre of our thinking. Is he *really*
that important?

Man is important not because he
thinks he is, but because God has
made him so. Part of the problem
of the general unsatisfactoriness of
life comes when man makes himself important *without* any reference to God. A simple question
and answer from the Westminster
Shorter Catechism* puts the Christian view of man neatly:

● **What is the chief end of man?**
● **Man's chief end is to glorify
God, and to enjoy him for ever.**

Life ought not to be about suc-
cess and fame, fun and finance. It
ought to be all about God, who is to
be the centre of my life. What I

think, say and do should all be
controlled by this thought: God
created me so that I might glorify
him, and enjoy him for ever.

Christianity insists that life will
make sense only when it is related
to God. The logic is straightforward. If life has to be summed
up, assessed, between the two terminuses of my birth and my death
it will never make sense. Life *isn't*
fair. The right word to describe it *is*
'unsatisfactory'. But once I allow
God to enter into the account, new
hope comes. It becomes possible
for my life to make sense. The
whole of life, the whole of creation,
can make sense.

Humanism recognizes the
unfairness of life and simply says:
'Life isn't fair. It's sad, but that's
the way it is. Just accept it.'

Buddhism says: 'Life isn't fair,
but that's because you don't recognize it for what it is: illusion,
maya. The suffering is illusion.
Individuals are illusion.'

Christianity says 'Life isn't fair,
but open your eyes and your life to
God. You are no mere cosmic accident, but unique. God made you so
that you might glorify him, and
enjoy him for ever. Be reconciled
to God and you'll be changed. As
this happens, the world will
change, too. *Then* take another
look at life!'

Before we can look at this idea of
being reconciled to God, however,
we must look at Jesus, who makes
that reconciliation possible.

---

*An agreed question-and-answer guide
to the Christian faith prepared at
Westminster in 1648 for the covenant
(or Presbyterian) churches of England,
Scotland and Ireland.

2

Jesus — the answer

The world's religions may be thought of as a collection of attempts to supply answers to the basic questions: 'Who am I?', 'Where did I come from?', 'Where am I going to?', 'Why?', and so on. For example, as Gautama the Buddha thought about human existence he was struck particularly by the universality of suffering. He proposed that we could escape from suffering by taking a middle path: not to be over-disciplined, nor yet to be undisciplined; not to laugh too much, nor yet to be permanently in floods of tears. Or take the answers provided by Karl Marx, where the problems of life originate in the class system. If we eliminate class from society, then the unfairness will gradually disappear.

For Christianity, the answers to the basic questions come through God's self-revelation generally in the Bible, and specifically in Jesus.

The name 'Jesus' is itself important because of its meaning: *'The Lord saves'* (see Matthew 1:21). The name presupposes a situation from which people need to be saved, and indicates that God has a means of saving.

Jesus was also known as 'The Christ'. This word is the Greek equivalent of the Hebrew 'Messiah', and both words mean 'anointed'. In Hebrew culture a person was anointed with oil as a sign that he was being called to some special task. Kings were anointed, as were priests and also prophets. In the case of Jesus it would seem that his work made him all three: prophet, priest and king.

When Jesus the Christ offered to those who would listen to him *his* answers to the basic questions, he did so in an entirely new way. Gautama the Buddha had investigated life, meditated on its mysteries and then offered his solution, but left God out of his system. Later on Muhammad would face the perennial questions, and he would claim that God *revealed* the answers to him. In the case of Jesus, however, we have something entirely different: Jesus claimed to have come from God, and to be God.

Buddha relief in a Hindu Temple, Java

The Jesus story

The life-story of Jesus has an unusual beginning, and an out-of-the-ordinary conclusion. (We would expect that if he were God.) Jesus had a human mother, but no human father. The unique story of the life of Jesus on earth starts with a unique act of conception: Jesus was born of a mother who was a virgin.

The story is told simply in Luke's Gospel. The angel Gabriel is sent to Mary to tell her that she is to give birth to a son, whom she is to name 'Jesus'. He will be known as the Son of the Most High God. Mary, understandably, is perplexed, and responds: '*I am a virgin. How, then, can this be?*' (Luke 1:34, GNB).

It's worth noting that Muhammad knew of this account of the birth of Jesus, and he recorded Mary's words to Gabriel as: 'How can I have a son when no mortal has touched me?' (*Qur'an*, Sura 19, verse 20).

Fulfilment of prophecy

In the Bible account, the evangelist Matthew explains this miracle as a fulfilment of a prophecy made long before by Isaiah (see Matthew 1:22–23). The prophecy occurs in Isaiah chapter 7. At the time the prophecy was made the Israelite kingdom was divided. Pekah was king of the northern part, Ahaz of the southern part. Pekah joined up with Rezin, king of Syria, and the two attacked Ahaz. Jerusalem was besieged. Isaiah prophesied, however, that the two kings would very soon give up the siege, and return to their own countries:

. . . the Lord himself will give you a sign: a young woman who is pregnant will have a son and

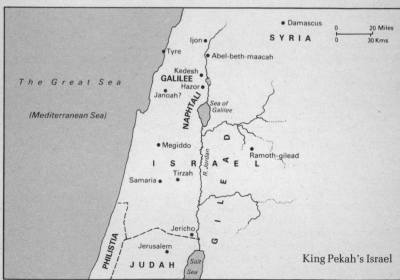

King Pekah's Israel

will name him 'Immanuel.' By the time he is old enough to make his own decisions, people will be drinking milk and eating honey. Even before that time comes, the lands of those two kings who terrify you will be deserted (Isaiah 7:14–16, GNB).

Like a good many other prophecies found in the Bible, this prophecy had two points of fulfilment: one near the time when the prophecy was made and a second, hundreds of years later. The first fulfilment came in Isaiah's day, somewhere around 730 BC. The siege of Jerusalem was on, a young woman had a baby, and before that baby could grow up enough to make his own decisions, to choose between good and bad, tasty and nasty, right and wrong, the besieging armies were gone.

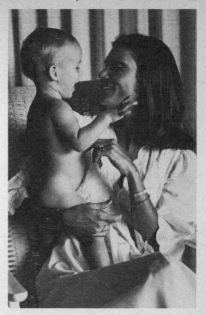

Mother and child

Isaiah, however, had used two very interesting words in his prophecy, one referring to the mother and the other referring to the child. The word he used for the mother *could* mean just a young woman. That's how the Good News Bible translates it. But the word *could* mean a virgin. That's how Matthew takes it, and when Matthew wrote his Gospel he wrote it in Greek, and he translated Isaiah's word by the Greek word *parthenos*, which clearly means 'virgin'.

Now the second word. Isaiah said that the child would be called 'Immanuel', which means 'God with us'. When Semitic peoples name their children they often use a name that is a comment on some event connected with the baby's birth. I remember a baby named 'Late harvest', because he was born when his parents were rather old. In the case of Isaiah's prophecy,

the name Immanuel was given to the baby because of the miraculous deliverance of Jerusalem from the attacking kings. The besieging armies heard of trouble back at home, and off they all went . . . and hence 'Immanuel', 'God with us', God who was on the side of the people of Jerusalem, and dealt with their enemies.

The full meaning of the prophecy, however, appears only in its fulfilment in Jesus. Jesus really was 'God . . . with us'. He was not merely a sign that God was on our side, but was, himself, God . . . with us.

The prelude to the account of the life of Jesus on earth, therefore, is important. There is a unique beginning, prophesied seven hundred years earlier. This shows God stepping into the world he had created, neither as some kind of superman, nor as a king, but as a miraculously conceived baby: God . . . with us.

Clearly, this view of the birth of Jesus is very different from that of those who see Jesus simply as a man. They see him as maybe a particularly good man, maybe a remarkable teacher, but still, just a man, interpreting and explaining the world as he found it. By contrast, the Bible presents a *unique* man, not one whose birth marks the beginning of his existence, but a man who steps into this world from the world beyond, from eternity. Indeed, this is what Christians mean by the *incarnation*. It is God becoming man, coming into the world he had created almost, yet *not*, in the normal human way. There is a unique beginning to a unique event.

His childhood

Jesus was born into a poor family. Mary, his mother, eventually married Joseph, a carpenter, and it seems that later they had several children. The evangelist Mark refers to Jesus' mother and brothers and sisters (see Mark 3:31–32). We know very little about his childhood. Probably he went with the family to Jerusalem each year. We know that he went there when he was twelve years old, and astonished the teachers of the law by some of the questions he asked them, and by some of the answers he gave to their questions (see Luke 2:46–47).

It is interesting to note the way in which, during that visit to the capital, Jesus gently corrected a slip of the tongue by Mary. When the party from Nazareth started to go home again, Jesus was left behind. Mary and Joseph then had to go back to the city to find him. When eventually they did, Mary was very upset.

'*Son, why have you treated us like this? Your father and I have been anxiously searching for you.*'

'*Why were you searching for me?*' *he asked.* '*Didn't you know I had to be in my Father's house?*' (Luke 2:48–49).

'Your father and I.'
'My Father's house.'

Growing-up

It's likely that Jesus spent long hours watching Joseph at work, making stools, beds, axe-handles, yokes for the necks of the oxen that

'For my yoke is easy . . .'

did the ploughing. Maybe that's the background to his gentle invitation, given many years later:

> Come to me, all you who are weary and burdened, and I will give you rest. Take my yoke upon you and learn from me, for I am gentle and humble in heart, and you will find rest for your souls. For my yoke is easy and my burden is light (Matthew 11:28–30).

His ministry

At about the age of thirty, Jesus chose a small group of twelve followers, and began some three years of almost incessant travel over the five thousand or so square miles of Herod's kingdom. As he went he taught and healed.

Jesus as preacher

The Jewish teacher, or 'Rabbi', was not merely a lecturer. He expected his students to absorb his total lifestyle, and to learn his teaching by heart. Jesus seems to have followed their example. The twelve followers of Jesus were expected to leave their jobs as fishermen or whatever, to follow their Rabbi.

Yet Jesus was different from other Rabbis. He was, and his followers knew that he was, both teacher and Lord: 'You call me "Teacher" and "Lord", and rightly so, for that is what I am' (John 13:13). It was not just his own followers who recognized that he was different from the usual run of Rabbis. The ordinary people recognized it too. The Rabbis did not claim any authority for themselves: they always quoted other Rabbis from the past as their authority for any rulings that they made. Jesus didn't:

When Jesus had finished saying these things, the crowds were amazed at his teaching, because he taught as one who had authority, and not as their teachers of the law (Matthew 7:28–29).

One of the great themes of Jesus' teaching was *God's kingdom*. Right at the beginning of his Gospel, Mark says that Jesus

> *... went into Galilee, proclaiming the good news of God. 'The time has come,' he said. 'The kingdom of God is near. Repent and believe the good news!'* (Mark 1:14–15).

This remarkable theme is a reminder to us that the world is not out of control; God rules over it. But this rule of God does not mean that we have no freedom. We are not like clockwork machines, wound up by God and doomed to carry on our amusing tricks until the clockwork runs down. Rather, we are free, and yet, like it or not, we live in a world ruled by a King.

Our situation is rather like living in a country where the government knows all about every case of law-breaking. No-one can even exceed the speed limit without the authorities knowing. So efficient is the government that every law-breaker is known, caught and punished. Now in such a country the people would be free, free even to break the law, and yet they would know that if they chose the way of crime they would have to take the consequences.

Of course it's an imperfect analogy. But it does indicate a very different picture of the world from that of, say, Hinduism, where I am not free. In Hinduism my condition and my actions today are the result of *karma*, the inescapable 'balance-carried forward' of my past. The debits and credits not only of my past in *this* life, but also in all my other previous lives, inescapably determine my life today.

The world picture painted by Christianity is also different from that of Islam, where the rule of God is taken to be absolute. Surely the most commonly heard phrase in all Arabic is the phrase *inshā' Allāh*, 'if God wills'. Certainly the most famous and the largest of the Muslim Schools of theology, the Ash'arite, deny human freedom and teach an all-embracing determinism.[1]

Picturing God's kingdom

When Jesus spoke of the kingdom of God it was to invite people to recognize God's rule, to submit themselves to it, not because of the privileges that would be theirs, but in recognition that he is *God*. The Jews had misunderstood God's message to them. They had seen it as giving them special privileges, as though God cared for them and

for no-one else, as though God's rule was for them alone. Eventually national pride led to national disaster. When Jesus was there, speaking of God's kingdom, the Jews were not free. They were part of the Roman empire. As always in such circumstances there were hopes that they might be free again. Rebellion? Revolt? Jesus reminded them of what they had long forgotten in their preoccupation with politics. He reminded them of God, and of the kingdom of God.

Matthew, chapter 13, contains seven parables about the kingdom of God. A parable is a story that can be understood, and then used to explain a truth that can't so easily be understood. These seven parables illustrate what Jesus had to say about God's kingdom.

● **He told of a man sowing seed.** Obviously the results depended on the kind of ground that the seed fell into: soft, rich, prepared soil; weed-infested ground; ground trampled hard by people walking over it; rocky ground. There's the first thing that Jesus has to say about me and the kingdom of God. If my heart is hard, bitter, filled with pride and self-sufficiency, then even if the good seed comes to me, even if I hear about the kingdom of God, I won't want it.

● **He told of the farmer who planted good seed, and then, during the night, an enemy came and sowed weeds in the same field.** When the good seed sprouted and the weeds also began to grow, there was no way that his labourers could pull up the weeds without also damaging the main crop. Here is an answer to those who won't come into the kingdom because of the mixture of people they see who claim to be part of it. The weeds might have claimed to be part of the main crop, just because they shared the same field. It is quite true that amongst God's people we also find cheats, liars and exploiters, weeds planted among the good seed; fine churches spoilt by the presence of hypocrites; honest Christians shamed by the presence among them of immoral people. Jesus warns us: that's the way it is, for now. The *real* nature of the kingdom won't be known until harvest time, until the judgment day when weeds are separated from the good grain, when hypocrites are set apart from faithful believers.

● **He told of treasure hidden in a field, and of a merchant looking for fine pearls.** The merchant was ready to pay anything to buy a really beautiful pearl. No price would put him off. It is true enough, we can't *buy* the kingdom of God; but there is a price to be paid for joining it. People don't understand, labelling you as a religious fanatic: all this God-talk is so *strange!* Our honesty may well make some of the people around us uncomfortable. In a society where integrity and honesty are rare, their presence is a continual rebuke to everyone, and so we may lose friends. In some parts of the world it could be far more serious: joining the kingdom of God may mean the loss of a job, the end of liberty, imprisonment, even death. In these two parables, of treasure hidden in a field and of the merchant looking for pearls, Jesus is suggesting to us: you may have to pay a high price if you come into the kingdom . . . but it's worth it!

● **Jesus told a parable about fishermen and their catch.** No doubt his listeners had often seen the fishermen of Galilee coming ashore with their nets filled with fish of all kinds. Then they would sit on the shore and sort out the good from the bad. Said Jesus, that's how it will be when the King comes to take up his kingdom, a time for sorting things out. The good is received, the bad thrown out. *That's* when it will all make sense. Built into this parable there is a warning: there really *is* a kingdom to enter, a heaven to win . . . a hell to shun.

● **Two other parables are included by Matthew in his collection of seven, the parable of the mustard seed, and that of the yeast.** The tiny mustard seed grows into quite a bush, big enough for the birds to nest in. The yeast, worked into the dough, exerts its raising power right through the dough. The kingdom of God had small beginnings. (Maybe Jesus had in mind that little uninfluential group of followers of his.) But wait until you see the end of it all! When the King comes back, then you'll know the extent of his kingdom! The people of the kingdom are comparatively few and apparently unimportant, but they are sent out into all the world as Christ's witnesses. The power of God is at work in them and around them . . . and the world is changed by them.

Jesus' emphasis on the kingdom of God helps to explain the answers to the basic questions given in chapter one. Where did I come from? Where did you come from? Where did this world come from? God made us and it. Both are *his.* Where are we all going to? Things are not out of control, heading for a smash, but leading to the time when the King will show himself as king, and gather his people into his kingdom. The rest? Like the weeds of the field, like the rubbish caught in the nets of the fishermen, they will be rejected, thrown out.

Jesus and his miracles

The gospels describe how Jesus cured people who were ill, brought dead people back to life, changed water into wine at a wedding, walked on the surface of the Sea of Galilee, commanded a storm to cease, and fed thousands of people with a few loaves of bread and some fish.

The stories are told simply and without apology. The miracles are performed in response to some particular need, never merely to prove that Jesus could perform miracles. The assumption always seems to be: 'This is Jesus. Of course he did these marvellous things. He is different. He is God . . . with us.'

We may identify three characteristics of miracles, they are:

● amazing,
● significant,
● demonstrations of power.

● **They are** *amazing* **because miracles are** *different***; there is nothing in ordinary life to compare them with.** So, when Jesus cured a man of paralysis, just by a sentence: '. . . *take your mat and go home*', the response of the crowds who saw it was predictable:

> Everyone was amazed and gave praise to God. They were filled with awe and said, 'We have seen remarkable things today' (Luke 5:26).

● **The miracles were** *significant*. They weren't trivial conjuring tricks. In the miracle of the healing of the paralysed man, Jesus used the occasion to talk about sin, and how it can be forgiven. He gave a vivid illustration of his own power, and pointed to his power in healing as an indicator of his unique power in moral matters.

Notice that the miracles didn't prove that Jesus was God with us. Many other people in both Old and New Testaments performed miracles, even brought people back to life. (There was Elijah in 1 Kings 17:17–23, Elisha in 2 Kings 4:8–37, Peter in Acts 9:32–42 and Paul in Acts 20:7–12.) But the miracles were significant. John comments after the turning of water into wine at the wedding in Cana:

> He thus revealed his glory, and his disciples put their faith in him (John 2:11).

● **The miracles demonstrated Jesus' *power*.** This strand is particularly important in Jesus' miracles of exorcising demons, and it relates to the theme we have already looked at – the kingdom of God. Jesus made it clear that there is *another*, evil power, opposed to the kingdom. Man is in the hands of the one power or of the other. Demons represent one of the agencies of the evil power. They are no figment of the imagination, fancies which the educated man may safely reject like Father Christmas. They were then a reality, and are still so today. Miracles occurred in which these evil powers were dismissed, and so dismissed by a *greater* power. In Luke, chapter 4, Jesus is in the synagogue in Capernaum. There was a man there who was demon-possessed. Jesus ordered the evil spirit to come out of him, and the demon obeyed. Again the response of the crowd is significant:

> All the people were amazed and said to each other, 'What is this teaching? With authority and power he gives orders to evil spirits and they come out' (Luke 4:36).

Perhaps understandably some people today find it difficult to believe in miracles. The objections seem to take three forms:

● 'I've never seen a miracle'
● 'Miracles are simply perfectly ordinary events exaggerated'
● a pragmatic assertion 'Miracles cannot happen'.

We'll look at these three objections.

● **I have never seen a miracle, and as a consequence simply don't believe in such events.** The argument gains a certain amount of strength if I can go on to say that none of my friends has ever seen a miracle, either. However we tend to find that if we do expand the number of witnesses we appeal to, we are likely rather quickly to be forced to modify our original denial. This is because, in a large circle of friends, we are likely to find someone who *has* seen or experienced something like a miracle, something he would actually label as such. For example, although I personally have never witnessed a miracle, two of my friends have, both miracles of healing. One was a cancer which simply disappeared, the other a baffling illness which defeated the doctors, put my friend off work for weeks, but which was simply dismissed, immediately, by the prayer of a friend who went to visit him. If I were not a Christian, or if I did not believe in miracles, therefore, I could say with confidence that I have never seen a miracle, but I might have to modify my statement if I included my friends, and say something like, 'I have never seen a *real* miracle, and neither have any of my friends', and by using the word 'real' I have excluded healing 'miracles'.

In fact, inexplicable healings and healings in response to prayer seem to have occurred with some regularity throughout history. The theologian Philip Melanchthon was brought back from the very edge of death through the prayers of Martin Luther, who wrote to his wife on 2 July 1540:

> . . . Philip was verily dead, and, like Lazarus, has been raised from the dead. God, the dear Father, hears our prayers. This we can understand, although we often do not believe it.

John Wesley, in the eighteenth century, was involved in a rather odd healing incident. He was on his way to a preaching appointment when his horse went lame. Wesley records that he dismounted, laid his hands on the horse and prayed for healing. The lameness went!

This argument, 'I have never seen a miracle and so miracles don't happen', is weak because there are so many things one hasn't seen; strong because it contains no ifs or buts; stronger still if I can add that none of my friends has ever seen a miracle either. In fact, asking my friends soon leads to someone who *has* witnessed something that certainly seemed like a miracle. But that's exactly what we would expect. Miracles *are* unusual events, so you would expect to have to look around a bit to find one. But they do seem to be there . . . if you look.

● **Miracles are merely natural events that have been exaggerated.** This second argument is that Jesus did not *really* feed five thousand people with five loaves of bread and two fish. What *really* happened was that the boy mentioned in the story brought out his packet of sandwiches and offered them to Jesus to see if they might help with the problem of feeding all those people. Then when the rest saw him do that they were ashamed and brought out *their* packets of sandwiches too. They'd been hiding them for fear that they would be expected to share them and there might not be enough to go round. Jesus didn't *really* walk on the water. What *really* happened was that he was walking along the shore. In the storm, and amidst the flying spray, and the sound of the howling wind, the people who were in the boat *thought* that Jesus was walking on the water.

I think it is reasonable to point out that the *only* evidence we have about these two events, the feeding of the five thousand and Jesus walking on the water, is the evidence of the Bible. There is no ambiguity about either story. Jesus is depicted as feeding five thousand people with five loaves of

bread and two fish. Jesus *is* shown walking from the shore to join his followers in the small boat which was in the middle of the lake (see Mark 6:45–53). Now it is entirely open to people who read these stories to say that they simply don't believe them. But if we do reject them we must beware of a certain danger:

> What we may not do is to invent something to put in the place of what we reject. There is an analogy here with those sceptics who find that they cannot believe the biblical account of the trial, death and resurrection of Jesus and undertake to tell us instead 'what actually happened'; Caiaphas was *really* trying to save Jesus, it was all *really* part of a Zealot plot, Joseph of Arimathaea *actually* took Jesus down alive from the cross, etc. There is no harm in such conceits as long as they are recognized for what they are, sheer fiction. But anyone who takes them seriously is more credulous than the most naive believer in the biblical text.[2]

Believe the stories or else don't believe them. But it is simply dishonest to pretend that they *don't* say what everyone knows they *do* say.

● **Miracles can't happen.** The simple assertion of this third argument is that people *can't* walk on water

and so they *don't*. To walk on water would be contrary to the laws of physics. We know the relevant laws quite well and experimental evidence confirms the laws. To which the Christian might respond: but laws are just deduction from observation. If I observe someone walking on the water then that observation must somehow be taken into my formulation of the law. Or the Christian might respond: yes, there are laws governing the affairs of nature and they are not accidental. God built them in when he created the world. And there surely isn't anything surprising about the fact that from time to time he transcends those laws. Or again we might observe that the universe is not quite the law-ridden thing that some of us imagine it to be. Physicists know that when we start to probe the fundamentals of the universe all the nice, tidy, understandable laws seem to dissolve and turn into questions of probability, of what *might* and *probably will* happen, rather than what *must* happen.

Shifting views of the universe

Actually it is worth while pausing to draw attention to an important series of changes that have occurred in our thinking about our universe. Before the seventeenth century the world was something of a chaos

> ... in which witches and demons, angels and 'Acts of God' might intervene at any moment ...

a world which was replaced by a world of law with

> ... an ordered sequence of cause and effect. By the end of the

nineteenth century that picture had become universal . . . The laws of science were as the law of the Medes and Persians which altereth not; an absolute rigidity conditioned man's whole nature, physical, mental and moral. In such a world there was no room for freedom, responsibility or standards of good and evil . . .*

There has been a third stage, however, in the series. Instead of abstract rules formulated about *things*, rules which simply ignored the people who weighed and measured the things, Einstein showed us a world characterized by the word *relativity*. Everything was to be interpreted, understood, in terms of the *observer*. Lengths, masses and velocities were not the absolutes we had thought them to be. They were relative to *us*. It is worth noting here that linguistics blindly followed science in its mechanical period and tended to dismiss man, who used the language, from the description of language. Noam Chomsky, the leading expert in linguistics of modern times, ruled *meaning*, semantics, out of court; it was not part of the study of language. That stage, too, has passed. Once again man is brought back in as being a central feature in scientific study.

In science Einstein was followed by others. Heisenberg introduced his principle of indeterminacy, that precisely because we can't know of an event without observing it, and because our observation immediately interferes with the event, there is an uncertainty built into all observation of fundamental processes. Professor C. E. Raven* again:

The recognition that there is a constant but unpredictable element of variability in the whole order of nature transforms the cast-iron sequence of the old concept into a process in which change and creativity can and do occur. *The difference between the two . . . may be quantitatively minute: it is philosophically immense.*

So the Christian might respond to the person who will not believe in miracles: a little more humility is called for on your part. You refer to the laws of physics. Very well: God put them there. You refer to what can and cannot happen: do we yet know what is, and is not, possible? Are we yet in a position to tell God what he may and may not do? You say that you have never seen a miracle. There are many things that you have not seen and maybe cannot ever hope to see without faith, without a surrender to God who alone makes sense of the world he has created. Trust therefore in Jesus, who reveals God to us, and who once demonstrated the power of God as he lived among us.

The Jesus story begins with a miracle, his birth from a virgin, and it reaches a climax in a miracle, the resurrection, and the miracles in between are signals, shouting peremptorily: 'Stop! Look! Think! Who *is* this man?'

To help us answer that question we turn now to the crux of Christianity. Not the life of Jesus, nor the miracles of Jesus, but his death.

---

*Professor C. E. Raven in an address to the 1953 Convention of the Institute of Physics, published in their Bulletin, July 1953.

3
Victory or defeat?

The facts

The basic facts are straightforward. Through the three years or so of Jesus' public teaching there was a growing hostility from the religious leadership. Just before the annual Passover celebration, Jesus was arrested by the Jewish authorities and accused of blasphemy. He was handed over by them to the Roman authorities, but freshly accused of sedition, in particular of 'speaking against Caesar'. The Roman Procurator, Pilate, sentenced him to death. He was crucified. After six hours hanging on the cross he died.

In a house in Calcutta a Hindu placed around the walls of one room key phrases from the world's religions. From Buddhism there was the mystical, 'Hail to the jewel in the lotus'; from Islam the invocation, 'In the name of God, the merciful, the compassionate'; and from Confucianism the aphorism, 'The sage relies on actionless activity'. Hinduism was represented by *Tat tuam ati*, 'That thou art.'

There was one biblical text, found in both Old and New Testaments. It was this text which was perceived as somehow lying at the heart of the Christian faith: Christ's words from the cross:

> *'My God, my God, why have you forsaken me?'* (Mark 15:34).

Christianity would commend the perception of that Hindu. Here, in the death of Jesus, is the key to the understanding of Christianity.

It is significant that the four gospels place their emphasis not on the life of Jesus, not on his parables, nor even on his miracles, but on the last phase of Jesus' time on earth.

John, for example, devotes some 45 per cent of his Gospel to the events of the last week of Jesus' life, 18 per cent to the account of the death and resurrection of Jesus.

Because of the approaching Jewish holy day, the Sabbath, his body was taken down from the cross and placed in a rock tomb. There was no time for the customary anointing of the body with the appropriate oils, spices and ointments. His followers, and especially the women amongst them who would be responsible for the anointing, had to content themselves with carefully noting the location of the tomb so that they would be able to return as soon as the Sabbath was over, to carry this out.

The tomb was closed in the traditional way by a large stone, rolled across the entrance. The Jewish authorities placed a guard over the tomb because they knew of Jesus' promise that he would return from death. Despite all these precautions, when the women arrived at the tomb at daybreak on the Sunday morning with their ointments, spices and oils, the tomb was empty.

Then for some forty days, in an entirely unpredictable way, Jesus was seen by various people. (Paul gives an impressive list of them in 1 Corinthians 15:3–8.) So far as we know he appeared only to believers. And then, after forty days, these appearances abruptly ceased. Some of his followers actually saw him taken away from them:

> . . . *he was taken up before their very eyes, and a cloud hid him from their sight* (Acts 1:9).

The case against Jesus

Jesus was born in Bethlehem, in the south of the country. King Herod heard of this 'King of the Jews' through wise men from the East, possibly from Persia (modern Iran) or Arabia. Fearing a rival king, Herod sent soldiers to kill all male children in Bethlehem, but Joseph and Mary were warned in a dream and fled with the child to Egypt. Eventually they were able to return to Nazareth, and there Jesus grew up.

Now Jewish history was remark- able because of the regular appear- ance of prophets, God's messen- gers, men who spoke out for God, and who not infrequently spoke out concerning future events. There had been Elijah and Elisha, whose names we have already met. There was Isaiah and his contem- porary Hosea. Malachi was the last of these prophets. After Malachi there was an ominous break in the line of prophets, rather more than four hundred years of silence. The voice of John the Baptist broke the

A desert scene at the foot of Mount Sinai

silence, announcing the coming of Jesus:

> After me will come one more powerful than I, the thongs of whose sandals I am not worthy to stoop down and untie. I baptise you with water, but he will baptise you with the Holy Spirit (Mark 1:7–8).

John had identified himself with an ancient prophecy. He was, he said,

> A voice of one calling
>   in the desert,
> 'Prepare the way for the Lord,
>   make straight paths for him'
> (Matthew 3:3 and see Isaiah 40:3).

John was the voice; Jesus was the Lord.

The people seem to have been quick to grasp John's message. Someone was at hand, at the very least a deliverer. Perhaps it was one who would be able to free the Jewish people from their Roman conquerors. God had given such men in the past . . . could this be the long-expected Messiah, the one anointed by God, deliverer of his people?

We saw in chapter two that Jesus was called the Christ (Greek) or the Messiah (Hebrew), both of which mean 'anointed'. We also saw there that kings were anointed, and so were prophets and priests. Granted that Jesus was the Christ, the Messiah, was he the anointed King, the anointed priest or the anointed prophet?

Deliverer: Messiah

In the Old Testament God is seen as raising up deliverers for his people. The book of Judges is the best illustration of this, with a long succession of deliverers such as Othniel and Ehud, the woman Deborah, Gideon and Samson. In

the prophecy of Daniel (9:24–27) we find the only Old Testament references to an un-named, future Messiah-deliverer. Out of this prophecy, and out of a recognition of God's role in the history of the nation in providing a deliverer, there came the strong Messianic expectation of the Jewish people.

Deliverer: Suffering Servant

However, there was a second strand of prophetic teaching in the Old Testament, focusing on a suffering Servant of the Lord. It was Isaiah, principally, who developed this theme. There are four passages in Isaiah which are sometimes called the *Servant Songs* (42:1–4; 49:1–6; 50:4–9 and 52:13 – 53:12). However there are other references to this Servant, seventeen in all (from Isaiah 41:8 to Isaiah 53:12). The fourth song, especially, pictures not a conquering Messiah but a suffering Servant.

Who was this suffering Servant? Professor G. B. Caird[1] puts it very clearly:

> Was the servant to be the whole nation or only a remnant, to be many, few or one? The reason

why modern scholars have endlessly debated these questions is that the prophet himself did not know the answers. It is as though he had published an advertisement, 'Wanted, a servant of the Lord', accompanied by a job description. He was undoubtedly aware that many famous men, such as Moses and Jeremiah, had sat for the composite portrait he was drawing. What he could not know was that in the end there would be only one applicant for the post.

The suffering Servant was to be Jesus.

So there were two strands of teaching in the Old Testament, each promising a deliverer, but one strand offering a King-Messiah and the second offering a suffering Servant. The Jewish people, oppressed by political tyranny, grasped at the identification of Jesus as King Messiah.

Jesus gave them no encouragement in this mistaken idea. Indeed, he repeatedly warned his followers against it, urging them to play down this identification of himself as Messiah. While it was right in principle, it was wrong in application. He *was* God's deliverer. But the disciples, no less than the masses of the people, seemed capable of thinking of deliverance only in terms of political liberation. In fact they were *still* thinking that way even after his death and resurrection. They asked him then:

Lord, are you at this time going to restore the kingdom to Israel? (Acts 1:6).

Well, Jesus didn't. He had come for a different purpose.

Yet it was obviously impossible to conceal his unique power. He healed . . . and who could stop those who were healed from talking about it? He raised the dead . . . and who could prevent the witnesses spreading the news? He told them not to (see Mark 5:43), but even so news of his power spread: even King Herod heard about him (see Mark 6:14). It was inevitable that Jesus should be seen as a threat to the religious leaders, whose lives could not match the simplicity, openness, and honesty of Jesus' life and who, in spiritual matters, lacked power. He was seen as a threat, also, by the political leaders, who saw in Jesus a danger to political stability.

Jesus had consistently refused this political role for himself. Take the example of the story in John 6. All four of the Gospel writers record this miracle of the feeding of the five thousand. *Of course* the people recognized the miracle, and inevitably they began to discuss the question of just who this Jesus was, and it was again inevitable that their thoughts would turn to prophecies of a deliverer. After all, there was a well-known Old Testament promise of a prophet like Moses who would be sent (Deuteronomy 18:15–19). Moses had miraculously given the people food, in the desert lands of Sinai. Was this the promised prophet like Moses? It must be!

Surely this is the Prophet who is to come into the world (John 6:14).

Their immediate intention is to make him king. Jesus knows it:

Jesus, knowing that they intended to come and make him king by force, withdrew again into the hills by himself (John 6:15).

Jesus refused to play politics. He had come as the suffering deliverer to challenge Satan not as a political deliverer to challenge Caesar.

The trial of Jesus

Jesus was never formally tried by the Jews. They no doubt intended all along to ensure that the Romans took the responsibility for his death. However an informal hearing was held:

> The chief priests and the whole Sanhedrin were looking for evidence against Jesus so that they could put him to death, but they did not find any. Many testified falsely against him, but their statements did not agree (Mark 14:55–56).

The question

Eventually the priests wearied of this unsatisfactory approach and they asked him outright.

Are you the Christ, the Son of the Blessed One? (Mark 14:61).

The question was an important one.

For one thing, it faced Jesus directly with the question of whether he was, or was not, the Messiah, the Christ.

For another thing, the high priest had used the strongest possible form of address in putting his question, so that Jesus was required to answer clearly.

I charge you under oath by the living God (Matthew 26:63).

Thirdly, the question was important because it gave to Jesus the opportunity of making clear to sophisticated theologians exactly who he was, what he meant by 'Messiah'.

His answer

I am . . . and you will see the Son of Man sitting at the right hand of the Mighty One and coming on the clouds of heaven (Mark 14:62).

What Jesus did in his answer was first of all to make his claim to be Messiah quite clear. Then he explained it not by the past (the virgin birth, the teaching, the miracles), but by reference to the future, to a forthcoming event prophesied by Daniel (see Daniel 7:13–14).

It seems to me that Jesus was making it quite clear that even those ideas of his Messiahship which were already circulating amongst the people fell far short of the reality. He was not merely a Messiah-king in the political sense. He was not merely 'the Son of the Blessed' in a figurative sense, God's messenger. He was claiming to be much more. The Daniel prophecy makes this clear:

> In my vision at night I looked, and there before me was one like a son of man, coming with the clouds of heaven. He approached the Ancient of Days and was led into his presence. He was given authority, glory and sovereign power; all peoples, nations and men of every lan-

guage worshipped him. His dominion is an everlasting dominion that will not pass away, and his kingdom is one that will never be destroyed. (Emphasis mine)

This response of Jesus, referring to a well-known prophecy, was a devastating response. No theologian could possibly doubt what Jesus was claiming. The high priest at once realized that Jesus was claiming to be more than mere man; he was laying claim to deity. This was blasphemy.

'Why do we need any more witnesses? . . . You have heard the blasphemy. What do you think?' (Mark 14:63–64).

The verdict

The response was unanimous: they all condemned him as worthy of death.

Of course the Romans would not be much interested in a prisoner accused of an offence against Jewish religious ideas. In fact, when the Jews first took Jesus to Pilate, he responded entirely predictably.

Take him yourselves and judge him by your own law (John 18:31).

Throughout the formal trial before Pilate, the Roman authority, there was this tension: he was being charged with blasphemy? Well, the evidence for this is fairly clear: let the Jews deal with the matter. He is being charged with sedition? Well, there seems to be no evidence for that; I will release him.

Ultimately it was a veiled threat from the Jews that resulted in the death sentence they wanted:

'If you let this man go, you are no friend of Caesar. Anyone who claims to be a king opposes Caesar.'
When Pilate heard this, he brought Jesus out and sat down on the judge's seat at a place known as The Stone Pavement (John 19:12–13).

And there he sentenced Jesus to death. If Caesar were to hear that a man claiming to be king had been arrested, accused, tried and released . . . the presiding judge would have a great deal to explain. Pilate dared not take the risk. Jesus must die.

Jesus on the cross

They crucified Jesus at nine o'clock in the morning. From the cross he spoke seven times. First, he pardoned those who drove in the nails. Then he made provision for John, one of his followers, to care for Mary, his mother. He also made a promise to one of the two political prisoners crucified with him that they would be together, in Paradise, that day. There was the cry, 'I am thirsty' and, lastly, there was the triumphant announcement: 'It is finished.' There was the traditional Jewish prayer at the end of the day: 'Father, into your hands I commit my spirit.'

And there was the central cry, the key to the whole event,

'My God, my God, why have you forsaken me?' (Mark 15:34).

the words that the Hindu put up on the wall of his room in Calcutta.

The seven words from the cross

The central saying is recorded by Matthew and by Mark, using the precise Aramaic words that Jesus used:
  'Eloi, Eloi, lama sabachthani?'

'Father, forgive them, for they do not know what they are doing'
Luke 23:34

'Dear woman, here is your son' *'Here is your mother'*
John 19:26–27

'I tell you the truth, today you will be with me in paradise'
Luke 23:43

'Eloi, Eloi, lama sabachthani?' Matthew 27:46
'My God, my God, why have you forsaken me?' Mark 15:34

'I am thirsty'   John 19:28

'It is finished'   John 19:30

*'Father, into your hands I
commit my spirit'*
Luke 23:46

Psalm 22

These words are the opening words of Psalm 22, written about a thousand years before the time of the crucifixion. Despite the long time-interval the Psalm provides a remarkable commentary on the experience of crucifixion. It might have been written for the event.

The Jewish understanding of Psalm 22 is usually that it refers to the collective sufferings and the eventual deliverance of the whole nation, although there have been suggestions that David's own periods of suffering, possibly when Saul was hunting him, were in mind. Certainly the Psalm would have had some immediate reference-point when it was first composed. Christians, however, would see the Psalm as also prophesying Christ's sufferings.

The Psalm falls into two parts:

- verses 1–21, with the theme of undeserved suffering
- verses 22–31 with the theme of praise for deliverance.

In the middle of the Psalm there appears to be a change of key, from the minor to the major. Applied to the event of the crucifixion the Psalm provides remarkable confirmation that Jesus *was* delivered from his awful experience of being alone:

> . . . *he has not despised or disdained*
> *the suffering of the afflicted one;*
> *he has not hidden his face from him*
> *but has listened to his cry for help* (verse 24).

However we are still left with the question: what was the reason for what is generally called Christ's 'cry of dereliction'? Why should Jesus feel himself abandoned by his Father? The answer supplies one of the central truths of Christianity: at his crucifixion Jesus was made '*to be sin for us*' (2 Corinthians 5:21); '*He himself bore our sins in his body on the tree*' (1 Peter 2:24); '*he was pierced for our transgressions, he was crushed for our iniquities*' (Isaiah 53:5).

Psalm 22:1–24

'My God, my God, why have you forsaken me?
  Why are you so far from saving me,
  so far from the words of my groaning?
O my God, I cry out by day, but you do not answer,
  by night, and am not silent.

Yet you are enthroned as the Holy One;
  you are the praise of Israel.
In you our fathers put their trust;
  they trusted and you delivered them.
They cried to you and were saved;
  in you they trusted and were not disappointed.

But I am a worm and not a man,
    scorned by men and despised by the people.
All who see me mock me;
    they hurl insults, shaking their heads:
'He trusts in the LORD; let the LORD rescue him.
Let him deliver him, since he delights in him.'

Yet you brought me out of the womb;
    you made me trust in you
    even at my mother's breast.
From birth I was cast upon you;
    from my mother's womb you have been my God.
Do not be far from me,
    for trouble is near
    and there is no-one to help

Many bulls surround me;
    strong bulls of Bashan encircle me.
Roaring lions tearing their prey
    open their mouths wide against me.
I am poured out like water,
    and all my bones are out of joint.
My heart has turned to wax;
    it has melted away within me.
My strength is dried up like a potsherd,
    and my tongue sticks to the roof of my mouth;
    you lay me in the dust of death.
Dogs have surrounded me;
    a band of evil men has encircled me,
    they have pierced my hands and my feet.
I can count all my bones;
    people stare and gloat over me.
They divide my garments among them
    and cast lots for my clothing.

But you, O LORD, be not far off;
    O my Strength, come quickly to help me.
Deliver my life from the sword,
    my precious life from the power of the dogs.
Rescue me from the mouth of the lions;
    save me from the horns of the wild oxen.

I will declare your name to my brothers;
    in the congregation I will praise you.
You who fear the LORD, praise him!
    All you descendents of Jacob, honour him!
Revere him, all you descendents of Israel!
For he has not despised or disdained
    the suffering of the afflicted one;
he has not hidden his face from him
    but has listened to his cry for help.

It must be emphasized that we are here at the very heart of Christianity.

Christianity is not only an analysis of man's problems together with some suggestions as to how *we* might solve the problems. Christianity is essentially what *God* has done about our problems.

Christianity stands or falls by certain historical events, not only by what Jesus *said*, but by what he *did*. Paul makes this entirely clear in his letter to the Corinthian Christians:

> For what I received I passed on to you as of first importance: that Christ died for our sins according to the Scriptures, that he was buried, that he was raised on the third day according to the Scriptures (1 Corinthians 15:3–4).

Now it is precisely at this point, at the most crucial point, that the world's religions conflict with one another. Judaism would deny that Jesus was the Messiah, that he died, and was raised to life again 'according to the Scriptures'. Islam would go even further and deny that Jesus was crucified; a Muslim scholar summarizes the conflict:

> The Qur'an, however, does not accept that he was crucified, but states that he was taken directly to heaven. This is the one

The open Qur'an

irreducible 'fact' separating Christianity and Islam, a fact which is in reality placed there providentially to prevent a mingling of the two religions. All the other doctrines, such as the question of the nature of Christ or the Trinity, can be understood metaphysically in such a way as to harmonize the two perspectives. The question of the death of Jesus is, however, the 'fact' that resists any interpretation which would be common to the Christian and Islamic views of the event[2]

I think that this is a very fair summary of the situation. For the sake of completeness it ought, perhaps, to be added that not all Muslims share the same view of the crucifixion. By far the majority have the view presented by Nasr. The Ahmadis, however, accept that Jesus was crucified, but reinstate an old idea, teaching that he merely swooned on the cross, revived in the tomb and eventually died in Kashmir.

Either interpretation of the crucifixion of Christ, however, contradicts the core teaching of Christianity: Christ died for our sins. The result of such contradiction is well expressed by an Ahmadi writer, Muhammad Zafrulla Khan[3]:

> Once it is established that Jesus did not die on the cross, there was no accursed death, no bearing of the sins of mankind, no resurrection, no ascension and no atonement. The entire structure of church theology is thereby demolished

He is quite right.

It must be said at once that there is no way of removing the idea of Christ's atoning death from the Bible by simply dropping a few

verses out, here and there. The Muslim world is taught that Old and New Testaments are corrupt, but if that is so it must at once be said that removing the corruption would mean very nearly the loss of the entire Bible, so deeply embedded is this doctrine of the atonement, the doctrine that my sins can be forgiven because Christ died for me. It is illustrated in the Old Testament through the story of the Exodus, and the sacrifice of the Passover lamb. It is illustrated in the complex system of sacrifice that pointed towards the eventual fulfilment of the system in the death of Christ. It is illustrated in the amazing story of the substitution of a ram to be sacrificed in place of Abraham's son, on Mount Moriah, in Genesis 22:1–14; in Isaiah 53 and Psalm 22; and in the institution of the Day of Atonement in Leviticus 16.

The fact is that Christianity takes sin seriously. It is far more than the wrong things that I do; sin is a principle, a power within me that dominates me. Now there are religions which suggest that all we need is education: once we know how we should behave then we shall be able to behave that way. Christianity, as it were, smiles grimly and replies: You can't!

We will easily recognize the reality and power of sin once we are aware of its full scope. God's judgment of my life takes in my thoughts, my motives, my desires, as well as my actions. Our legal systems can't deal with thoughts, only with such acts as stem from the thoughts. But God takes note of the wrong thoughts and the wrong actions and sees them both as flowing from a sin principle, a *power* operating in us all. And it is worth asking ourselves: is Christianity right or wrong in its analysis? Can I, in fact, do what I *ought* to do; can I even do what I *want* to do?

Sin is a reality. Few people would even bother to attempt to deny it. The cross lays emphasis on a second aspect of the sin question: God's righteousness. Both Old and New Testaments agree in this: God cannot simply say to us: 'We'll forget about your sins.' Sins have to be dealt with. In the Old Testament period there was a system of animal sacrifices. Those sacrifices never did deal with the sins. What they did was to point forward to the eventual means of dealing with sin in Christ. Century after century passed by with only a symbolic dealing with sin. It might have appeared that sin went unpunished and righteousness went unrewarded. Then Christ came to deal with all sin, the sin of those who lived in Old Testament days, and of those who have lived since. There is no difference: all sinned, and all sin is dealt with in the one way:

There is no difference, for all have sinned and fall short of the glory of God, and are justified freely by his grace through the redemption that came by Christ Jesus. God presented him as a sacrifice of atonement, through faith in his blood. He did this to demonstrate his justice, because in his forbearance he had left the sins committed beforehand unpunished (Romans 3:22–26).

They weren't left unpunished, however; ultimately Jesus dealt with them all.

Of course the picture of Christ's death as a sacrifice is only one picture that is used in the Bible. There is also the very powerful illustration of slavery. Jesus himself gave us this picture:

> For even the Son of Man did not come to be served, but to serve,

Captives being sent into slavery

and to give his life as a ransom for many (Mark 10:45).

This idea of slavery is particularly strong in Paul's letter to the Romans, probably because they would have been very familiar with slavery. (It was likely that some of the Christians at Rome were themselves slaves.) Paul comments that the Roman Christians were, once, 'slaves of sin' (see Romans 6:17 and 20), but had been set free by Christ. Peter makes it even clearer:

> For you know that it was not with perishable things such as silver or gold that you were redeemed from the empty way of

life handed down to you from your forefathers, but with the precious blood of Christ, a lamb without blemish or defect (1 Peter 1:18–19).

Notice here that Peter actually puts the two illustrations together: redemption from an inherited slavery to sin, and freedom through the death of Christ who is compared with a sacrificed lamb.

There are other illustrations used in the Bible, aimed at explaining or at least at throwing some light on the meaning of the death of Christ.

What the Bible does not allow us to think is that the crucifixion of Christ was simply a ghastly mistake, a terrible miscarriage of justice, a travesty of all legal process. It was not the Romans who killed Jesus, nor was it the Jews. Jesus 'lay down' his life and insisted that he had power to do just that . . . and to take up his life again (see John 10: 17–18).

In the earliest Christian sermon recorded we find one of Jesus' first followers, Peter, saying:

> This man was handed over to you by God's set purpose and foreknowledge; and you, with

the help of wicked men, put him to death by nailing him to the cross (Acts 2:23).

The crucifixion of Jesus was not an accident. It was the central event of all history. It is the one indispensable key to understanding Christianity. It is the key to the Christian answers to the basic questions.

Just as ultimately those basic questions are personal questions (who am I? where did I come from? where am I going to? why?), so the key is a personal one. It is a key offered to you as you come to the end of this chapter. The key will fit the lock only so long as it keeps its original shape. Twist the key, bend it, cut it about and the key won't fit, the door remains locked, life remains a mystery, death keeps its terror. But accept the key as the Bible offers it to you and God comes in Christ, having offered up his life for your life: Christ the Man without sin loaded down with your sin and nailed to a cross; Christ crucified, dead, buried for you. Take that as the key and the door swings open. The whole Jesus story, the very history of the world, life, your life, all make sense.

Here's something to do, now. Read the story for yourself, in Luke's account, from chapter 22, verse 47, to the end of the book. Luke wrote a second book, Acts. Carry on reading with the first chapter of Acts. See what has happened to Peter: a new man! Read through his sermon in the second chapter. See the realization dawning on those people in Jerusalem: *they* were responsible for the death of Jesus. *Their* sins sent him to the cross . . . 'Brothers, what shall we do?' (Acts 2:37).

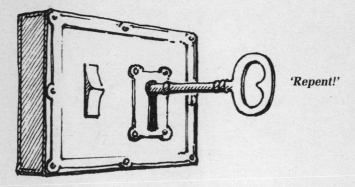

'Repent!'

4

Jesus alive!

'Woman,' he said, 'why are you crying? Who is it you are looking for?'

Thinking he was the gardener, she said, 'Sir, if you have carried him away, tell me where you have put him, and I will get him.'

Jesus said to her, 'Mary.'

She turned towards him and cried out in Aramaic, 'Rabboni!' (John 20:15–16).

'Rabboni!', 'My Rabbi', 'My teacher'!

Jesus was crucified at nine o'clock in the morning, died at three o'clock in the afternoon and was hastily taken down from the cross and buried in a nearby tomb. Saturday, the Jewish 'Sabbath' day of ceasing from work, began at six o'clock in the evening, so that there was no time for the customary preparation of the body before burial.

Mary

Early on Sunday morning a group of women went to the tomb with spices, oils and ointments to anoint the body. They found the tomb open, the body gone. And then followed a long series of appearances of Jesus to his followers. The very first was at the tomb itself only minutes after the women had made the momentous discovery of the empty tomb. Mary Magdalene, one of Jesus' followers, was still standing there, outside the tomb, weeping, simply not knowing what could have happened to the body. Notice this: she did *not* expect Jesus to be raised to life in this way. She produced an obvious explanation: someone had stolen the body ... maybe a final act of sadistic cruelty on the part of the Jewish religious leaders? Then came Jesus:

Thomas

Mary Magdalene was not the only one of the followers of Jesus who found it difficult to believe that he was alive from the dead. The story of Thomas is the story of one of the twelve apostles, the small group particularly chosen by Jesus to be near him and with him in his work. Even here the resurrection was not expected. Jesus appeared to the apostles on that first Sunday evening, in an upper room in Jerusalem. For some reason Thomas was not with them. When the rest told him that they had seen Jesus, that he was alive, Thomas refused to believe it:

'Unless I see the nail marks in his hands and put my fingers where the nails were, and put my hand into his side, I will not believe it' (John 20:25).

One week later Thomas had his wish. Once again the apostles were together, this time with Thomas, and once again Jesus appeared to them.

'Peace be with you!'

He gave the customary Jewish greeting, and then, turning to Thomas, made it embarrassingly clear that, although he had not been *visibly* present when Thomas had so forcibly announced his unbelief, still he knew:

> 'Put your finger here; see my hands. Reach out your hand and put it into my side. Stop doubting and believe' (John 20:27).

It seems clear from John's account of this incident that Thomas didn't need to put his fingers into the marks of the nails in Jesus's hands, nor to feel the wound in his side that had been made after his death by the spear of a Roman soldier. Thomas's response was immediate and extremely significant.

'My Lord and my God!'

This is an amazing confession by Thomas, a total surrender. Abandoning his unbelief, he acknowledges Jesus not merely as a human teacher or leader, but as God: 'My *Kyrios*, Lord; my *Theos*, God!'

But that's just Thomas! Surely he could have been making an emotional response? He was wildly wrong before in denying that Jesus had appeared to the other apostles; is this an equally wild response but in the opposite direction? It is, fittingly, Jesus himself who settles the question:

> Then Jesus told him, 'Because you have seen me, you have believed; blessed are those who have not seen and yet have believed' (John 20:29).

Jesus doesn't correct Thomas. On the contrary, this confession by Thomas is identified as an act of faith, 'You have believed'. Jesus' response here makes a striking contrast to that of an angel messenger sent to John in a vision many years later. John was guided through that amazing experience by an angel, and at the end of it all John was overcome by the things he had seen:

> And when I had heard and seen them, I fell down to worship at the feet of the angel who had been showing them to me.

Now notice the immediate response of the angel:

> But he said to me, 'Do not do it! I am a fellow-servant with you and with your brothers the prophets and of all who keep the words of this book. Worship God!' (Revelation 22:8–9).

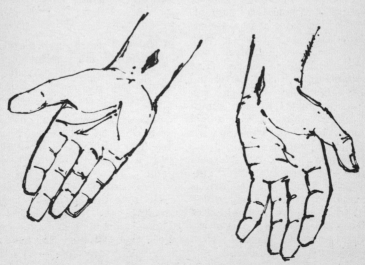

Alive!

That was precisely the response of the followers of Jesus when he appeared to them, alive! The appearances went on for forty days, their faith made stronger by every fresh appearance. And then came the day of his return to heaven:

> When [Jesus] had led them out to the vicinity of Bethany, he lifted up his hands and blessed them. While he was blessing them, he left them and was taken up into heaven. Then they worshipped him and returned to Jerusalem with great joy (Luke 24:50–51).

So we have two very interesting sides to the story of the resurrection of Jesus: there was an empty tomb and there was a live Jesus. Jesus' followers did not believe just because of the empty tomb: Mary explained that by supposing that someone had stolen the body. The religious leaders of the Jews explained it by saying that Jesus' followers had stolen the body. Some modern writers have explained it by saying that Mary and the others went to the wrong tomb. Jesus' followers believed, not because of an empty tomb, but because of a living Jesus. Peter saw him. The apostles saw him. Some five hundred of his followers saw him on a single occasion (see 1 Corinthians 15:5–7). And what is so important for us to notice is that Jesus appeared to people who did not expect to see him. These appearances can't be explained simply as self-delusion: 'They wanted to see him and so they eventually convinced themselves that they had seen him.' They did not expect him to come back to them, but he did. In fact John comments on the situation of the followers of Jesus even when they were confronted by the empty tomb:

> They still did not understand from Scripture that Jesus had to rise from the dead (John 20:9).

What convinced them was the irresistible evidence of a living Jesus.

The importance of the resurrection

The resurrection of Jesus, the certainty that he is alive, not dead, is vital to Christianity, not an optional extra. It is as important to know that he is alive today as it is to know that he died for our sins according to the Scriptures. Paul makes this clear in an entire chapter of his letter to the Christians at Corinth dealing with resurrection:

- If Christ has not been raised, our preaching is useless and so is your faith
- If Christ has not been raised your faith is futile; you are still in your sins
- Those also who have fallen asleep in Christ are lost
- If only for this life we have hope in Christ, we are to be pitied more than all men (see 1 Corinthians 15:12–19).

As Paul so clearly explains, the resurrection is the test of everything that Christ had ever said, taught, promised. The earliest of the four Gospel writers, Mark, tells us that Jesus had promised his followers that he would be killed, but rise again, back to life (see Mark 9:31 and 10:34). They didn't understand him, as Mark tells us:

> But they did not understand what he meant and were afraid to ask him about it (Mark 9:32).

Yet here was the ultimate test of the truth of what Jesus had said. Others had performed miracles before Jesus. Others had offered new explanations of the mystery of life. Indeed, in the so-called Mystery Religions which existed two hundred or more years *after* the time of Christ, and might have existed at the time of Christ in a similar form, there was even a legend of Osiris dying and then having the bits of his dismembered

Osiris as depicted on the tomb of Amenophis II

body re-assembled by his wife and brought back to life by magic. But *that* event, and other similar events in the Mystery Religions, was placed safely back in the dim and forgotten past: there were no witnesses to appeal to. When he wrote his letter to Corinth Paul had most of his four hundred witnesses to the resurrection of Jesus still alive!

Here was the ultimate test. Could Jesus fulfil his promise, to die and to rise again? The New Testament insists that he did. And it is again Paul who comments on the centrality of the resurrection. He writes about Jesus,

> ... who as to his human nature was a descendant of David, and who through the Spirit of holiness was declared with power to be the Son of God by his resurrection from the dead: Jesus Christ our Lord (Romans 1:3–4).

There was no question about Jesus' *human* descent through the line of David. The question concerned his claim to divine descent. What proof was there that he was the Son of God? Paul's proof is unequivocal: the resurrection.

Preaching the resurrection

The resurrection of Jesus was not a doctrine that somehow got borrowed from the so-called Mystery Religions, and was tacked on to Christianity later on. In fact, as Professor Bruce Metzger[1] has pointed out in his very careful study of the relationship between the Mystery Religions and Christianity, it is probable that the borrowing went the other way (*Historical and literary studies*. Sir Norman Anderson's[2] book *Christianity and World Religions* also deals with this issue.)

Peter

The resurrection was a central part of the preaching of the first followers of Jesus.

In that powerful speech by Peter on the Day of Pentecost, just ten days after Jesus had returned to heaven, Peter told the crowd:

'... God raised him from the dead, freeing him from the agony of death, because it was impossible for death to keep its hold on him' (Acts 2:24).

A few days later Peter referred to it again:

'You killed the author of life, but God raised him from the dead' (Acts 3:15).

In the very next chapter in Acts Peter and John are arrested by the Temple guard:

They were greatly disturbed because the apostles were teaching the people and proclaiming in Jesus the resurrection of the dead (Acts 4:2).

The following day they were taken before the High Priest, and the other religious leaders of Jerusalem, and again their theme was the resurrection; how had they been able to heal a cripple?

'If we are being called to account today for an act of kindness shown to a cripple and are asked how he was healed, then know this, you and everyone else in Israel: It is by the name of Jesus Christ of Nazareth, whom you crucified but whom God raised from the dead, that this man stands before you completely healed' (Acts 4:9–10).

They were threatened but set free and returned to the other Christians to give their report on what had happened. The writer of Acts summarizes the consequence:

With great power the apostles continued to testify to the resurrection of the Lord Jesus ... (Acts 4:33).

In chapter 5 of Acts we find the apostles arrested, put in prison, and the prison doors are opened for them by an angel. Once again they are out in the Temple courts talking about Jesus! Re-arrested, they are again questioned by the High Priest, and again the insistent testimony comes across:

'The God of our fathers raised Jesus from the dead – whom you had killed by hanging him on a tree. God exalted him to his own right hand as Prince and Saviour...' (Acts 5:30–31).

The resurrection is part of the Christian answer to the basic questions that we looked at in chapter one.

Yes, life is unsatisfactory and doesn't make sense. The mess that the world is in is not God's fault, as though he had lost control of it, but our fault, the consequence of sin dominating our lives. There's no way in which by some great universal determined effort we can overcome sin. We know by sheer hard experience that old habits are stronger than new year resolutions, that in spite of every intention of being better we are not better. What we need is for someone to come and to deal with sin.

Sin is the problem. Christ is the answer: not Christ the example, nor Christ the miracle-worker, nor Christ the teacher, but Christ crucified, dead, buried, risen, ascended, alive! It is Christ today in the place of power, able to set us free from our slavery to sin, able to give us new life, a fresh start, our past forgiven, our future assured.

This discovery of Christ is the greatest discovery any of us can ever expect to make. Without him we are desperate indeed, lacking resources to deal with the *real* problems of life. They overwhelm us. Finding Christ is sudden, marvellous relief: at last, the Man who can cope.

I remember a good many years ago taking my daughter to school. As I rounded the corner into the road where the school was, there on the pavement were two figures amid a pool of blood. Horrified, I hurried my daughter into school and rushed back across the road. The couple lying there had, as I later learnt, been living together. They had argued violently that morning. He had pursued her down the road, sunk a kitchen knife through her back and into her heart. He then pulled out the knife and slit his own throat. He wasn't yet dead. With another man I set to work to see if anything could be done to save their lives. Someone had gone to telephone for an ambulance and the police. But we had to try something ... heart massage, the kiss of life, staunch the flow of blood ... something. What enormous relief it was after some minutes to look up and see a policeman, an ambulance and a doctor ... and I could put the whole sorry mess into the hands of people who could cope.

It's a poor illustration of what we Christians have experienced: a sudden, deepening awareness of the enormity of the problem posed by life – it's *such* a mess – with the growing realization that we couldn't cope, and the relief when Jesus, the Man who cares and copes, came into the situation.

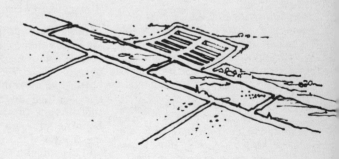

5

New life!

people demanded ... '...*what shall we do?*'. Peter's response was quick and clear: '*Repent and be baptised*...' (Acts 2:37–38).

Baptism was an acted parable, a public witness. It was a parallel to Christ's death and resurrection, the water representing the grave: alive *out* of the water, into the water to symbolize death, out of the water again into life, but this time into resurrection life, life shared with Jesus who is alive! It's all there in Romans 6:3 4:

The resurrection of Jesus was immediately seen by the first Christians as being absolutely central to the good news. Only if Jesus were alive could there be any good news to preach. If death had beaten *him*, then it could still beat *us*. But if he came through, then we might come through. His resurrection life had a new quality about it, a new power in it. Well, then, we could share it!

Very quickly the Christians adopted baptism in water as the outward sign of admission to the church. In fact, right on the Day of Pentecost, in Peter's first public preaching of the good news, the

> ... *don't you know that all of us who were baptised into Christ Jesus were baptised into his death? We were therefore buried with him through baptism into death in order that, just as Christ was raised from the dead through the glory of the Father, we too may live a new life.*

That's what we have always wanted; power to live a new kind of life; resurrection power to beat temptation, to speak the truth! Christianity is *not* a theory, or a system, or a philosophy, nor the wisdom of a dead teacher, but the power of a living Jesus. Its power is available to me!

A Christian baptism in Mali

The Holy Spirit

clear. Jesus was arrested, was tried, was executed, was buried, did return from death. Forty days later he did return to his Father in heaven. And after a further ten days he did send the Counsellor. The story of the coming of the Counsellor, the Holy Spirit, appears in Acts, chapter 2:

> When the day of Pentecost came, they were all together in one place. Suddenly a sound like the blowing of a violent wind came from heaven and filled the whole house where they were sitting. They saw what seemed to be tongues of fire that separated and came to rest on each of them. All of them were filled with the Holy Spirit... (Acts 2:1–4).

This power is brought to the Christian by the Holy Spirit. We'll have to leave a consideration of the meaning of the Christian Trinity to the next chapter, but we must now introduce the third remaining Person of the Trinity. God the Father we know. Jesus we know. Any further consideration of new life must focus attention on the Spirit .

Immediately before he was arrested, Jesus told his followers:

> 'It is for your good that I am going away. Unless I go away, the Counsellor will not come to you; but if I go, I will send him to you' (John 16:7).

The promise that Jesus made is quite clear. He was about to be arrested, tried, executed, buried. He would return from death and then go, again, to his Father in heaven. And from there he would send this Counsellor. The fulfilment of the promise is equally

Before and after

The rest of the book of Acts is essentially an account of what the first Christians did, their acts, as a result of being 'filled with the Holy Spirit'. Right from the beginning it is made clear that they were now people of power. When Jesus was arrested Peter had three times denied any relationship with him. After he was filled with the Spirit Peter is found openly preaching in the streets of Jerusalem, fearlessly standing up to the threats of the religious leaders, healing the sick, even raising the dead. The change was startling. When the religious leaders of the Jews had Peter and John arrested, and interrogated them, they recognized that something new, strange had happened to these fishermen:

> When they saw the courage of

Peter and John and realised that they were unschooled, ordinary men, they were astonished and they took note that these men had been with Jesus (Acts 4:13).

What had happened is simply explained. Before they were filled with the Holy Spirit they had been much like everyone else: liars, sometimes; proud, sometimes; violent, sometimes; but they were entirely unable to deal with their lying, pride and violence. There was an inevitability about their behaviour. There was a *law* operating from which they couldn't escape. But Christ's death *for them*, and the Spirit's coming *to them*, had set them free from that law. These two laws are referred to in Romans 8:2 as:

- the law of sin and death
- the law of the Spirit of life.

Two laws

Christianity offers us an analysis of our human predicament. We are all under just one of these two laws, either the law of sin and death, or the law of the Spirit of life. Perhaps the clearest explanation of *dukkha*, unsatisfactoriness, and the solution to it, appears in Paul's letter to the Christians at Rome. The letter has a very simple outline.

Now we plunge right into the heart of the letter to find the focus. Romans 8:2 states:

Paul's letter to the Christians at Rome: an outline		
1:1–17	Introduction	
1:18–3:20	Condemnation:	We have all gone wrong
3:21–5:21	Salvation:	How we may all be put right through Christ
6:1–8:39	Sanctification:	Natural man or spiritual man; a choice between two laws
9:1–11:36	Question:	Are the Jews a special case?
12:1–15:33	Application:	How to live in the power of the Spirit
16:1–27	Conclusion	

... *the law of the Spirit of life set me free from the law of sin and death.*

The law of sin and death

Two laws, and we operate under the one or the other. There are no other alternatives. Christianity teaches that the reason for the chaos in the world, the admitted unsatisfactoriness of life, is that people are living under *the law of sin and death*. We can identify this law for ourselves, frustrating all our attempt to be *good*. We must be realistic, here, brutally honest. Although it is true that everyone has moments of kindness, times when others are put first, still at heart we are all selfish. That concentration on self is the root of the law of sin and death. It means *me* and not *you*; it means *me* and not *God* as I plan my life, make my decisions.

Me first, everyone else very much second – this basic human way of thinking kills off every plan by the United Nations, or even by well-meaning governments. Frankly, the western nations won't take a cut in their standard of living so that the developing nations may improve theirs. The wealthy minority in Third World nations won't take a lower standard of living in order to benefit the hungry masses of their own people. We're all in this, all of us to blame, all of us essentially self-centred, all subject to this *law of sin*. Me first! Go to the headquarters of the Organization of African Unity in Addis Ababa. Count the Mercedes cars lined up outside. Watch the delegates from poverty-stricken African countries driving off to their luxury hotels – no different, really, from their western colleagues in Paris, Washington, Moscow, Rome, and the rest.

The law of sin is operating powerfully in our lives, so that we even shock ourselves by our selfish behaviour. The law of sin and death means the death of our high ideals, of our moral standards, of integrity, of any kind of relationship to God. Obviously we dare not develop a relationship with him … he *knows*. He knows *us*.

The law of sin and death is simply set out in Romans 7:15–25. I've used the paraphrase of the Living Bible, because it makes it all so clear. But here it is in summary:

- I really want to do what is right, but I can't.
- I know perfectly well that what I am doing is wrong.
- I can't help myself.
- I want to, but I can't.
- It seems to be a fact of life that when I want to do what is right, I inevitably do what is wrong.

If that is in agreement with your experience, then you agree with the Christian analysis of our human problem.

The law of the Spirit of life

Now for the alternative: *the law of*

Romans 7:15–25 (The Living Bible paraphrase)

I don't understand myself at all, for I really want to do what is right, but I can't. I do what I don't want to – what I hate. I know perfectly well that what I am doing is wrong, and my bad conscience proves that I agree with these laws I am breaking. But I can't help myself, because I'm no longer doing it. It is sin inside me that is stronger than I am that makes me do these evil things.

I know I am rotten through and through so far as my old sinful nature is concerned. No matter which way I turn I can't make myself do right. I want to but I can't. When I want to do good I don't; and when I try not to do wrong, I do it anyway. Now if I am doing what I don't want to, it is plain where the trouble is: sin still has me in its evil grasp.

It seems to be a fact of life that when I want to do what is right, I inevitably do what is wrong. I love to do God's will so far as my new nature is concerned; but there is something else deep within me, in my lower nature, that is at war with my mind and wins the fight and makes me a slave to the sin that is still within me. In my mind I want to be God's willing servant but instead I find myself enslaved to sin.

So you see how it is: my new life tells me to do right, but the old nature that is still inside me loves to sin. Oh, what a terrible predicament I'm in! Who will free me from my slavery to this deadly lower nature? Thank God! It has been done by Jesus Christ our Lord. He has set me free.

---

the Spirit of life. This new law relates to the Holy Spirit who filled the first Christians on the Day of Pentecost. When he moved into their lives they received new power. Jesus had dealt with the problem of sin, selfishness, pride and the rest. Now the Holy Spirit gave them power to be positive. Christianity is not merely a negative dealing with sin, but a positive empowering for a new quality of life, life in the Spirit.

Now Jesus had told his followers before his arrest that it would actually be better for them if he went away (see John 16:7). Of course they didn't believe him, then. But when the Spirit came they could see why it was better. Jesus went away but the Spirit came. When Jesus was with them he could be in only one place at a time. When he was with Peter, James and John up on a mountain in northern Judea, he couldn't be with the rest of his followers who were in desperate need of him down in the valley (see Luke 9:28–43). But the Holy Spirit isn't like that at all. He is not confined by a physical body and so he can be in Galilee and in Jerusalem, in Birmingham and in Madras, in Nairobi and in Lima.

This Spirit is the Spirit of life, always with the Christian, and always ready with power to live the new quality of life that Jesus promised to his followers. He shows us authoritatively what is true (see John 14:17) and what is not true (see John 16:7–8), and then he gives us what we never had before: power to do what is right, and *not* to do what is wrong.

Now let's be quite clear about this. God really does intend to 'make us good'. If Christianity can't produce *good* people then it's a sham. Ultimately the aim is to produce *perfect* people, an ultimate goal towards which we should be steadily growing. We grow toward this perfection as the Spirit steadily shows us his views on right and wrong, as he points out new sins which we had, perhaps, not even noticed previously. That's how it ought to be – with perfection finally realized in heaven.

Sin is a bit like an onion. An onion won't bring the tears to your eyes until the outer skin is peeled off. But then you peel the next layer and the tears roll. And the next layer ... and another ... and another. As you get deeper into the onion so the more your eyes run! Sin is like that. As you get to understand it better, so you feel its wickedness more profoundly. To change the metaphor, God's goodness is like a fire; the closer you get

to it, the hotter it seems. As we begin to grow spiritually and so to come closer to God, so we under-

stand and feel more his splendid goodness ... and to become aware of how far short of that kind of goodness we fall.

Sin! It's not just a vague theological idea, but it's a label for so much that is wrong, evil, depraved, oppressive. Just recently I was in Soho, London. A woman came out of a shop, dragging her child after her. He was maybe four years old, and obviously terrified. As she dragged him off, sobbing, down the street she was shouting at him: 'I'll kill you when I get you home.' That's sin, that had the child's life in ruins before it even had a chance to flower into something beautiful. But that's not all. What about the sin that had ruined the young woman's own life? What was it that had turned her life into such a hell? Only a few years earlier she had been a girl at school, running home to her mother, her father ... or was it that, her home, that had marked her? Or perhaps her marriage? I don't know. But that's sin, and that's what sin does. Life isn't merely 'unsatisfactory'. In so many ways it's far worse: it is appalling.

I've just been watching a video recording of the execution of thirteen former Government ministers in Liberia. They were forced to strip to the waist, bound to a long line of posts, then shot. But that's not the truly horrifying bit. Rather, it is the exultant attitude of the executioners, prancing triumphantly around the pathetic crumpled corpses, waving their automatic weapons in the air, that is horrible. I don't know what the crimes of the shot men were, but no one of us should *rejoice* over the death of another.

In a sense those pictures of sin encapsulate the law of sin and death. Jesus came to set us free from it, and to lead us into the law of the spirit of *life*.

Becoming a Christian

The Spirit doesn't make us into new people without our consent. The God who reveals himself in the Bible allows us the dignity of decision.

We may decide to keep him out of our lives altogether. We can do that. The thought of having him there, in the lounge, listening to our conversation, at work, watching the way we do things, at home, filling in the income tax declaration ... having *him* there would certainly demand some changes. Perhaps we're not willing to make those changes.

But if we *are*? If the analysis offered here so far makes sense, if I can see this appalling evidence of sin, not just in the world, but in *me*, personally, and if I can see that I'm unable to do anything about the law of sin and death ... what then? What can I do to move on to the new law, the law of the Spirit of life?

What must I do?

First of all, the answer to this question 'What can I do?' is not 'Nothing'. If I do nothing then I'll stay as I am.

Secondly, if I *want* to move into this new kind of life it's worth knowing that this of itself is evidence that God is seeking me. He is not merely seeking everyone in general, he is seeking *me*. It is he who has put this wish into my mind.

Let me explain this new thought. I've just been reading a book, *Christianity Rediscovered*, by Vincent Donovan. Donovan was a missionary to the Maasai people of East Africa. They taught him the real meaning of faith, the nature of the change which takes anyone into God's family. In explaining to the Maasai how to become a Christian he had used a word in their language which meant 'to agree to', rather as you might agree to the analysis of human life that I've suggested in this chapter. A Maasai elder put him straight:

He said for a man really to believe is like a lion going after its prey. His nose and eyes and ears pick up the prey. His legs

give him the speed to catch it. All the power of his body is involved in the terrible death leap and single blow to the neck with the front paw, the blow that actually kills. And as the animal goes down the lion envelops it in his arms (Africans refer to the front legs of an animal as its arms) pulls it to himself, and makes it part of himself. This is the way a lion kills. This is the way a man believes. This is what faith is.[1]

Now that's part of the explanation of what faith is, involving us. But the Maasai elder continued:

> You told us of the High God, how we must search for him, even leave our land and our people to find him. But we have not done this. We have not left our land. We have not searched for him. He has searched for us. He has searched us out and found us. All the time we think we are the lion. In the end, the lion is God.

And that's the second part of the explanation of what faith is. Ultimately we will realize that even the *desire* to be different was given to us by God. As the Bible puts it:

> ... *it is by grace you have been saved, through faith – and this is not from yourselves, it is the gift of God* (Ephesians 2:8).

Six vital steps

Even though ultimately it is God who gives us faith, however, the answer to the question 'What must I do?' is not 'Nothing'. New life won't come simply by passively waiting for the lion to pounce. So here are six ways in which the New Testament answers the question.

1 I must believe. I must accept God's explanation of this world, his explanation of why life is unsatisfactory and how Christ's death can put me right. I must believe in Jesus, accepting that he is more than a prophet, a teacher and a miracle worker, as Thomas did: 'My Lord and my God' (John 20:28).

2 I must be born again. This is what Jesus demanded of Nicodemus, the Jewish Rabbi. Like so many religious people Nicodemus thought he had all the answers. In fact he had to ask for a fresh start, one as radical as a new birth would be. The old worldview and way of life may have to go.

3 I must repent. Repentance in the New Testament means essentially a change of mind. If I am not sorry for my sins now, I can't become sorry without this change. I may be excusing my sins: 'They're not so bad. No worse than anyone else's sins. I do my best. No-one's perfect. In fact I'm probably a good deal better than some of these so-called Christians.' But I must change my mind, and repent.

Repentance is connected with *confession*. To confess my sins is to say about them exactly what God says about them. That's the literal translation of the Greek word 'to confess', *homologeō*, 'to say the same thing'. No excuses!

And along with the repentance and the confession there comes a determination; a desire, with God's help, to abandon those sins.

4 I must give up everything. Jesus put it starkly:

> If anyone comes to me and does not hate his father and mother, his wife and children, his

brothers and sisters – yes, even his own life – he cannot be my disciple (Luke 14:26).

Jesus has to come first, before everything and everyone else. Thus, it isn't easy to become a Christian. It may be desperately dangerous when a Marxist realizes that Jesus was far more than 'the first great communist'. It can be shattering when the Muslim realizes that Jesus was more than a prophet. The whole way of life may be affected when a Hindu puts Jesus on an entirely different plane from the gods of Hinduism. The rich man may find himself set to lose a fortune if he comes to Christ.

Jesus actually challenges us: weigh it up! Count the cost! If there is something, someone that means more to you than I do ... then you can't be my disciple.

5 I must follow Jesus. This means far more than simply trying to imitate Jesus. He lived in his century, we live in ours. It really isn't possible to try to live his way today. This is one of the real difficulties that the Muslim has in trying to follow, literally, the life-style of Muhammad. Times change. Customs change. You can't turn back the clock.

The fact remains that I must follow Jesus, as Peter and John and the rest of them did: Jesus is the Rabbi and I am the disciple; he is the master and I am the servant. He has the right to direct my whole life.

I must follow his example. He was humble, and so must I be. He cared for ordinary people, and so must I. He shared what he had with the poor, and so must I. He lived out his life in dependence on his Father, and so must I. He shared the good news with those he met, and so must I. I am not a follower of Martin Luther, John Calvin, Charles Spurgeon, or John Wesley; not a Lutheran, Reformed, Baptist or Methodist. I am a follower of Jesus.

6 I must receive Christ. John commented on Jesus:

He came to his own home, and his own people received him not. But to all who received him, who believed in his name, he gave power to become children of God (John 1:11–12, RSV).

John's picture of Jesus is clear. He came to the world that was his, and to the Jews who ought to have been his people. But they wouldn't have him. Yet far from abandoning us, Jesus still waits, offering himself and the new life which he can give to anyone who will receive him.

I must believe. I must be born again. I must repent. I must give up everything. I must follow Jesus. I must receive Christ.

It was Easter Sunday, 1947. I was sixteen years old, already out at work, as an office boy in London. Already I knew that life didn't make sense. Kneeling by a little table I surrendered to God, believing that Jesus was the Son of God. I was born again, accepting the new start Jesus promised me. So I began my walk with Jesus.

6
One God

words of the *Shema* ('Listen!'):

> *Hear, O Israel: the Lord our God, the Lord is one. Love the* LORD *your God with all your heart and with all your soul and with all your strength* (Deuteronomy 6:4–5).

Jesus actually designated this as the most important of all the commandments (see Mark 12:29). Yet right through the centuries the church has held on to its doctrine of the Trinity, one God in three Persons. It is a doctrine which is most easily perceived through three events: creation, the incarnation and Pentecost.

God has revealed himself in creation. It is possible to see in the world around us his 'God-ness'.

> *For since the creation of the world God's invisible qualities – his eternal power and divine nature – have been clearly seen, being understood from what has been made* (Romans 1:20).

Yet it is somehow difficult to see

Not three gods, one God. The Nicene Creed, a statement of belief which is accepted by the Anglican church, the Roman Catholic church, the Eastern Orthodox churches and by most Protestant churches, begins

I believe in one God.

Christians accept the authority and inspiration of the Old Testament as well as of the New Testament, and can stand with the Jewish people and repeat the

The created world: Three Sisters, Glencoe, Scotland

how the God who could make all that — not just this world, but all the other worlds out there in space — could possibly take any notice of me. After all, very few *people* have time for me . . . how could I expect God to take notice of me?

I made reference to Donovan's book *Christianity Rediscovered*[1] in chapter 5. He tells of a visit to America. He was talking to a group of young people in high school. He asked them to think about who would be affected if something really drastic happened to them. One girl asked,

'You mean if I committed suicide or something?'

When Donovan agreed that that was the kind of thing he had in mind, the girl thought a moment and then replied,

'Mary here, and my mother.'

No-one else? Just two people? This is an almost imperceptible ripple on the vast pool of life. Creation does reveal God's power and divine nature, but somehow it makes him so remote from us. He becomes the far-away God.

Once I talked with some African Christians about their old religion. It all seemed to focus on Doressa. He was the cause of every accident, every illness, every calamity. Doressa caused famine, withheld the rain, sent disease, held back the crops, produced deformity in babies. So all the attention of the people was directed towards Doressa. They offered him annual sacrifices and their ritual experts, their *shamans*, worked to keep Doressa contented. But they did know another God. Anthropologists who had studied these people had not heard about him. He didn't appear in their books and articles. According to the textbooks the people had a belief only

in the death-dealing Doressa. But that wasn't true. They also believed in Magano, creator of heaven and earth.

Magano, however, was far too great to be concerned with them. He was the High God, the Sky God. Having made the world, he had retired to his own distant retreat and had no dealings with the people he had created. When the first preachers of the good news about Jesus came to them they came preaching the traditional good news of the forgiveness of sin through faith in Jesus. But that wasn't the way the people heard the preaching. What came through to them was this amazing good news: Magano has come near! The same thing happened in Ruanda. The missionaries preached an orthodox gospel, but the people heard it rather differently: God has come near!

Sometimes I wonder if those of us who are Christians have not been at fault here. Christians don't seem to see that for most people the creator-God is so remote, so entirely uninvolved. The world is in chaos, with people dying of starvation in Bangladesh, suffering in their tens of thousands in the Sahel regions of Africa, battered by war in the Middle East, out of work in the once-prosperous West, at the mercy of all kinds of dictators in South America. Yet the God we speak of, the God of creation, seems to be a million miles away from it all. We may respond to his self-revelation in creation 'God is great', Allahu akbar, but we can't imagine him taking notice of us.

God understands all that. He has revealed himself in another way: through the incarnation, through Jesus. God made himself small, small enough to be seen and known in an entirely new way. He became a speck in a woman's womb, a baby born into a poor family in Palestine, a homeless refugee in Egypt, a wandering preacher with a handful of unin-fluential followers, a man denied justice, condemned to die on a wooden cross. And Christianity says: This is God! God come near!

The New Testament describes the incarnation of Jesus like this:

> Who, being in very
>   nature God,
>   did not consider equality
>   with God
>   something to be grasped,
> but made himself nothing,
>   taking the very nature of
>   a servant,
>   being made in human
>   likeness.
> And being found in
>   appearance as a man,
>   he humbled himself
> and became obedient to
>   death —
>   even death on a cross!

(Philippians 2:6–8).

At the time it must have been very confusing for Jesus' followers. They were all Jews. They had been taught to repeat the words of the Shema, 'The Lord is one', from childhood. Yet it was quite obvious that Jesus stood in some unique relationship to God. Jesus himself explained it to them:

'If you really knew me, you

Jewish boy reading Scripture for his Barmitzvah

would know my Father as well. From now on, you do know him and have seen him.'

Philip said, 'Lord, show us the Father and that will be enough for us.'

Jesus answered: 'Don't you know me, Philip, even after I have been among you such a long time? Anyone who has seen me has seen the Father. How can you say, "Show us the Father"? Don't you believe that I am in the Father, and that the Father is in me?' (John 14:7–10).

It seems to have been the resurrection that convinced the followers of Jesus that he was God incarnate, God come near. Thomas seems to have been the first to express it clearly, when Jesus appeared to him one week after the resurrection. Without attempting to work out the theology of it, Thomas put his belief into simple words:

'My Lord and my God!' (John 20:28).

Pentecost we have already looked at in chapter four. Before his arrest, Jesus promised that he would send another Counsellor (see John 15:26). The Counsellor would come, as Jesus had come, from the Father. Jesus described him as the Spirit of truth, who would guide his followers into the truth.

After his resurrection, and before his return to heaven, Jesus again spoke about this promised Counsellor:

'Do not leave Jerusalem, but wait for the gift my Father promised, which you have heard me speak about. For John baptised with water, but in a few days you will be baptised with the Holy Spirit' (Acts 1:4–5).

Who was this 'Counsellor'? The question is particularly important to Muslims, since Islam suggests that Muhammad was the promised Counsellor. However, two observations make it clear that Jesus could not have been referring to Muhammad.

● First of all, Jesus used the Greek word *paraklētos*, 'Counsellor'. The word is a legal word and means Counsel in a court of law. He could be Counsel for the prosecution or Counsel for the defence. Here in John's Gospel he is essentially Counsel for the prosecution, because he convicts, or convinces, unbelievers about the truth of the testimony of the believers:

'When he comes he will convict the world of guilt in regard to sin and righteousness and judgment' (John 16:8).

Some Muslim writers have confused the word *paraklētos* with a similar Greek word *periklytos*, meaning 'famous', 'renowned', 'praised', and have then related this to Muhammad, whose name also means 'renowned' or 'praised'. They have then suggested that Jesus was prophesying the coming of Muhammad.

● But, secondly, we have to note that Jesus promised his followers that this gift would be given to them *'in a few days'* (Acts 1:5). That statement certainly fits in well with the coming of the Holy Spirit at Pentecost just a few days after Jesus had made the promise, but cannot be made to fit the five hundred and forty or so years that would elapse before Muhammad was born.

Pentecost came fifty days after the resurrection and ten days after Jesus' ascension, his return to the Father. On the Day of Pentecost the third Person of the Godhead came with power to the followers of Jesus.

And there they are, Father, Son and Holy Spirit, most clearly identified in three events, creation, incarnation and Pentecost. The church has struggled with this mystery, trying to see if there might be some way of simplifying the doctrine of the Trinity. The fact is that there is no way of honestly understanding the evidence of the Old and New Testaments other than by this idea of the Trinity: one God, in three Persons.

The three Persons are presented in a single event at the beginning of Jesus' period of teaching. Jesus went to be baptized by John the Baptist and Matthew describes what happened:

As soon as Jesus was baptised, he went up out of the water. At that moment heaven was opened, and he saw the spirit of God descending like a dove and lighting on him. And a voice from heaven said, 'This is my Son, whom I love; with him I am well pleased' (Matthew 3:16–17).

Jesus himself spoke of the three to his followers:

'When the Counsellor comes, whom I will send to you from the Father, the Spirit of truth who goes out from the Father, he will testify about me' (John 15:26).

Paul made reference to the three when he wrote to the Christians in the city of Ephesus:

There is one body and one Spirit . . . one Lord, one faith, one baptism; one God and Father of all (Ephesians 4:4–6).

Baptism has from the beginning been the practice of the church, and each time a person is baptized, the command of Jesus is followed: they are baptized in the name of the Father and of the Son and of the Holy Spirit (see Matthew 28:19).

So the first Christians learnt to say 'Jesus is Lord', led by the Holy Spirit (1 Corinthians 12:3). They learnt to receive the Holy Spirit into their lives and so to enjoy the power that would enable them to live a new quality of life altogether, what the New Testament calls the life of eternity. But they left it to others to try to produce an

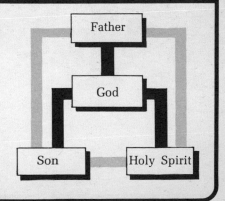

The Trinity

One way of showing the relationships between the three Persons of the Trinity. The outside paths are *forbidden* paths:

- The Son is *not* the Father
- The Spirit is *not* the Son
  The Father did *not* die on the cross
  The Son did *not* come at Pentecost

The inside paths are *open* paths:

- The Father *is* God
- The Son *is* God
- The Spirit *is* God

Father

God

Son

Holy Spirit

The Trinity: four illustrations

Each form does have the same essence: each is equally 'water'.
All three may exist together in equilibrium at the 'Triple point'

but . . .

this illustration does tend to direct attention to the heresy, the 'modalist' heresy, that Father, Son and Spirit are simply three modes in which God appears to us.

Water, which may exist in three forms
● liquid – water
● solid – ice
● vapour – steam

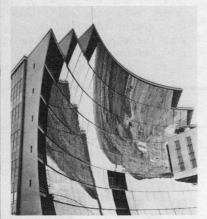

Attention is focused here on three ways in which the sun may be experienced: felt as heat, seen as light and used as a source of energy

but . . .

again there is no identity; heat is *not* the sun

and . . .

the recognition of heat, light and energy depends on the existence of an observer as though God would exist only if there were someone to *see* his Son or to experience the power of his Spirit.

The sun, which may be experienced as:
● heat
● light
● energy

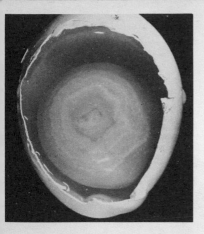

The egg is one egg, not three; each part has its distinctive role to play in the egg

but . . .

there is no *identity* in this illustration; the shell is *not* the egg, the yolk is *not* the egg in the sense in which the Son *is* God.

An egg, which has three principal parts:
- yolk
- white
- shell

No one of these three need be dominant and each of the three is equally *tea* and each of the three has its own distinctive contribution to make to the total 'tea'.

Tea, which may be a blend of, say, three types:
- India tea
- China tea
- Ceylon tea

explanation of the mystery of the Trinity.

There is a story that the theologian J. S. Whale used to give a series of lectures on the Trinity, in one of the Scottish universities. When he'd finished his course he used to ask his students,

'Now, have you got it?'

Always there would be some cheerful student who would reply

'Yes!'
'Well then,' Whale would retort, 'you've got it wrong!'

Which is my way of saying that I am not going to attempt to produce some nice neat way of explaining this profound mystery. Surely it ought not to surprise us, however, that God should turn out to be much more difficult to understand and explain than maybe we thought when we were just children.

C. S. Lewis illustrated the Trinity from mathematics. If we stay in one dimension we have a very simple system, simply a row of points. If we advance to two dimensions we keep all the properties of the one dimension, but now we can have lines which lie on a plane. If we go on to three dimensions we keep all the properties of points and planes, but now we can add solid figures: cubes or cones or whatever. The form of a cube, for example, demonstrates six planes and twelve lines and an infinite number of points and it has the three-dimensional property of spaciousness. But physics reminds us that we need not stop there. We can't *draw* them and most of us can't even imagine them, but we can add on more dimensions, four, five, fifty, if we like. And each

The Trinity

With just *one* dimension we hav points which might define a line

But physics opens up the way to understanding of more dimensions. Time may be added as a fourth dimension . . . and mathematical formulae can be produced to deal theoretically w more dimensions still.
Theoreticians begin to talk about multi-dimensional space-time continuum . . . which can't be dismissed merely because we do understand it!

an illustration from mathematics

With two dimensions the lines spread out to produce a plane

With three dimensions we produce 'spaciousness' as forms such as cubes become possible

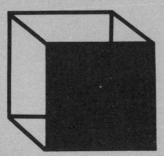

additional dimension allows us to retain all the properties we had before, but to add on more.[2]

So it is with our understanding of God. When we think of him simply as 'God', or 'Father', we are inclined to picture him as simply a super-man; but when we take hold of the Trinitarian picture, Father, Son and Holy Spirit, new understandings begin to become possible. We discern love in the Trinity, and power, pain, and intercession in ways that were simply not possible before.

Of course that doesn't mean that we now 'understand' God. But it opens up fresh ideas of just *how* great he is.

7

Taking God's Word for it

The Bible is really a library of sixty-six assorted books, poems and letters. It is possible to sort out the main historical books from the rest and so provide a reasonably continuous outline of history as the Bible presents it.

The Bible provides a history

The Bible *does* give us a history of the world, but it is a history as seen from a special viewpoint.

Of course that is true of *every* so-called history. What is usually taught in schools as 'history' is merely the history of political power and this is then presented as if it were the history of mankind. But as Karl Popper made shatteringly clear in his book *The Open Society and its Enemies*,[1] the history of power politics is one of international crime and mass murder, in which some of the greatest criminals are extolled as heroes. The history found in the Bible is very different. It is a history of unimportant people, and an insignificant nation, through whom God has gradually disclosed a plan for the salvation of the world.

The process of disclosure passes through two principal phases, corresponding to the Old Testament period and the New Testament period and beyond, relating firstly to the Jewish people and secondly to the church. There's an old story about Frederick the Great, who is said to have demanded proof of the existence of God. Quickly he was told, 'The Jew, your Majesty.' Certainly, the Jews are a remarkable people. For various reasons they seem to have suffered persecution century after century, with more than three million massacred in the Second World War, and yet they are still with us. The Old Testament is primarily concerned with their history; God chose to reveal himself through them. They were to be his servants, his messengers, to share their knowledge of him with the surrounding peoples.

Instead, the Jew usually was able to think only in terms of special privilege. Yes, God *was* their God, and their history showed that he had cared for them. Doubtless, he would continue to do so ... but it was all rather boring ... politics was much more exciting. So they lost sight of God's purpose in calling them. Isaiah chapter 65 has a striking illustration of God's unsuccessful attempts to get their attention, to call them back to their task:

> I revealed myself to those
>   who did not ask for me;
> I was found by those who
>   did not seek me.
> To a nation that did not call on
>   my name,
>   I said, 'Here am I, here am I.'
> (Isaiah 65:1).

This is a striking picture, daringly using the analogy of a common children's game 'sardines', we used to call it. One person hides, and the rest are expected to find him, then they all crush into whatever hiding-place he has chosen. But in *this* game the children have given up the search. They don't *want* to play. They are no longer

An Old Testament overview

Genesis	An account of beginnings: how it all began. The long history of Abraham, his children and grandchildren, explaining how they got to Palestine and then settled in Egypt.
Exodus	How Moses took them out of Egypt, where they had become slaves, and led them back to the very borders of Palestine again.
Joshua	A new leader, Joshua, takes over. An account of the way the twelve tribes, descendants of Abraham, settled back into Palestine.
Judges	An account of Joshua's successors, including Gideon and Samson, and how they repeatedly saved the nation from the surrounding peoples.
1 Samuel	Samuel is sometimes called the last of the Judges and the first of the great prophets. A new start: Saul becomes the first king. The story of the growing conflict between Saul and David, and the death of Saul.
2 Samuel	David becomes king. His long reign.
1 Kings	David is succeeded by Solomon. Solomon builds the Temple in Jerusalem. Rebellion led by Jeroboam. The nation divided on Solomon's death, only two tribes, Judah and Levi, remaining faithful to Solomon's son Rehoboam. The prophet Elijah.
2 Kings	Elisha succeeds Elijah. The succeeding kings of Israel, in the north, and Judah, in the south. Israel smashed, taken into exile. Judah struggles on, but they, too, go into exile, but to Babylon.
Ezra and Nehemiah	How the exiles from Babylon were allowed to return to Jerusalem, and how they rebuilt the city and the Temple.

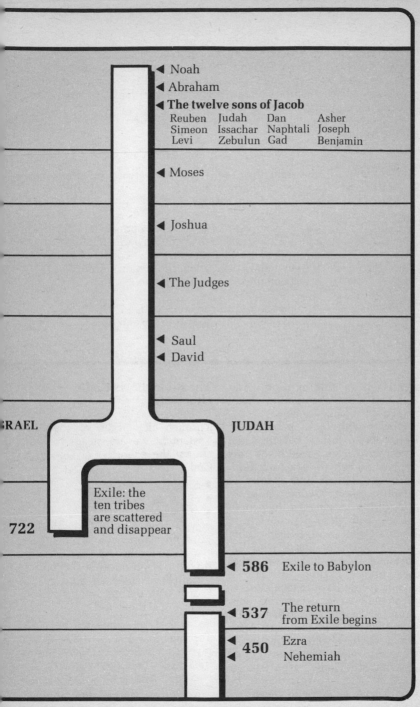

◀ Noah
◀ Abraham
◀ **The twelve sons of Jacob**

Reuben	Judah	Dan	Asher
Simeon	Issachar	Naphtali	Joseph
Levi	Zebulun	Gad	Benjamin

◀ Moses

◀ Joshua

◀ The Judges

◀ Saul
◀ David

ISRAEL   JUDAH

722   Exile: the
       ten tribes
       are scattered
       and disappear

◀ **586** Exile to Babylon

◀ **537** The return
           from Exile begins

◀ Ezra
◀ **450** Nehemiah

After Ezra and Nehemiah there is a gap of some 400 years in the historical record of the Bible. However there is a fascinating bridge between Old and New Testaments provided by the First Book of Maccabees, which records the events that affected Palestine after the death of Alexander the Great in 323 BC. In particular it describes the great revolt under Judas Maccabaeus about 166 BC. However 1 Maccabees is not one of the books of the Bible, but can be found in the Apocrypha.

Matthew, Mark, Luke, John	How John the Baptist, last of the great prophets, announced the coming of Jesus. Jesus' birth, life, teaching, death, resurrection.
Acts	The acts of the first Christians, empowered by the Holy Spirit. How the Christian church began in Jerusalem and spread northwards into Syria. And how Paul took the good news throughout the Roman empire. Paul's arrest and imprisonment in Rome.
Revelation	A remarkable epilogue. John, exiled for his faith, is given a vision of the events of the end time.

interested in finding God. And God, far from abandoning them, calls out to them: 'I'm here!'

It was with these people that God entered into a covenant, an agreement. They would be his people and he would be their God. Through all their long history of rebellion, idolatry, compromise, in spite of leaders who led the people astray, and people who chose leaders who would lead them astray, God kept steadily to the covenant. His justice meant that from time to time the Jewish people would have to face punishment. The exile, when the remnants of the twelve tribes were swept off to Babylon, and Jerusalem was left abandoned, in ruins, was clear enough confirmation of that. But still God's purpose never wavered. Through *this* people he would bring salvation to the world.

The Bible shows God's character

Through the pages of the Old Testament we are steadily being shown the character of God as a God

- of love
- of justice
- of creation
- who cares for the insignificant: for the poor, the widow, the orphan, for the nobodies.
- who has promised a Saviour, a Deliverer, someone who could deal with the misery, confusion and sin of the world.

So at last we come to the New Testament, and God's self-revelation in Jesus. As the writer of the letter to the Hebrews put it:

In the past God spoke to our forefathers through the prophets

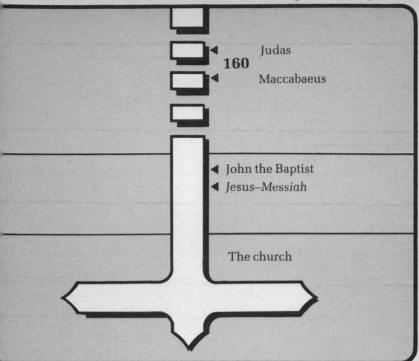

Judas
160
Maccabaeus

◀ John the Baptist
◀ *Jesus–Messiah*

The church

at many times and in various ways, but in these last days he has spoken to us by his Son (Hebrews 1:1–2).

The New Testament is an account of the life, death, resurrection and ascension of Jesus and of the church which grew out of the preaching of the good news about him.

The Bible is inspired

The Bible is a book of history, history written from a particular viewpoint: God's. The Bible is an *inspired* book, not merely the chance compilation of a collection of human authors. We must look a little more carefully, however, at what Christians mean when they speak of an inspired book. After all, most of the world's major

religions have their sacred books: the Qur'an for Islam, the Upanishads for Hinduism, the *Tripitaka* or 'Three Baskets' for Buddhism.

For the Christian, the concept of inspiration puts the responsibility for the total contents of the Bible, Old and New Testaments, back beyond the human scribes and on to God. But the human writers are not merely writers-down of dictation. Their individuality comes through. The Greek of John is not the same as the Greek of Paul. The Hebrew of Genesis is not the same as the Hebrew of Isaiah. We can go on to say that Paul's *style* comes through, and so does John's and Isaiah's. Behind them, nevertheless, is God.

The Bible is a written selection

This leads to a further important

observation: what is in the Bible is *selected* out of so much more that might have been there. John makes this quite clear:

> Jesus did many other miraculous signs in the presence of his disciples, which are not recorded in this book (John 20:30).

A process of selection has occurred and what is written down is there for a purpose. The collection of sixty-six books is not accidental.

The Bible is accurate

A third observation is that the inspiration of the Bible implies also its *correctness*. This point does from time to time lead us into some perplexity. There are places where the Bible appears to contradict what we know from some other source. When I was a student, for example, we were told that Jesus could not have grown up in Nazareth because there was simply no evidence at all, archeological or literary, to suggest that there had been any settlement on the modern site of Nazareth before the fourth century AD.

How, then, had the story that Jesus had lived in Nazareth appeared? The suggestion was that the idea that Jesus was a Nazirite, a 'holy man' (see Numbers 6:1–21), had developed in the early church and that idea had become confused with the name *Nazareth*. Or maybe there had been confusion over the prophecy in Isaiah 11:1 about a Branch (Hebrew *nitser*) and this had been misunderstood as Nazar and then again confused with Nazareth.

The Evidence

But in 1955 archaeologists were excavating under the Church of the Annunciation in Nazareth and found clear evidence that, in fact, the place had been occupied even *before* the Christian era. Then, in 1961, an inscription was dug up in Caesarea, from the period of the Roman occupation, which actually included in it the name of the town of Nazareth.

Take also the story of the crucifixion of Jesus. As a student I was told that when a man was crucified by the Romans he was not *nailed* to the cross, but tied to it. Thomas's request to put his finger into the nail-prints must have been a later fabrication by people who had never seen anyone crucified. But then in 1970 the bones of a man named Jehohanan were dug up. He had been crucified, and the nail which had been driven through his ankle bones was still in place and pieces of wood from his cross were still there! (These two examples come from A. E. Harvey's book *Jesus and the Constraints of History*[2].)

These are two apparent errors which have been resolved, and I have lived long enough to see many of my early problems on the *correctness* of the Bible sorted out for me. I am content to allow the scholars to work on those that still remain.

The Bible is reliable

The idea of inspiration carries with it a fourth assumption: that the Bible is not merely correct in what it records, but that the text which we have is *reliable*: it is what Paul, John and the rest wrote down centuries ago. Once we realize just how ancient some parts of the Bible are (parts of the Old Testament, for example, going back three *thousand* years), we realize

A Dead Sea scroll

also that even its existence is astonishing. We do have very old manuscripts to work from when we wish to check the text. There are more than five thousand manuscripts in Greek, containing all, or part, of the New Testament. Probably the most exciting discovery in this area of Bible documents in recent years was the discovery of the Dead Sea Scrolls. Scholars now tend to refer to them as the Qumran Scrolls, because we now know that they belonged to a community which lived in Qumran, not far from the caves where the Scrolls were found. These Scrolls consisted mainly of books of the Old Testament; in fact almost every book of the Old Testament was represented in the collection of Scrolls. They were written somewhere around the time when Jesus was there in Palestine, maybe a hundred years earlier, maybe a few years later.

Making use of these manuscripts of Old and New Testaments, scholars are able to check the text

of the Bible that we use, and to assure us that the text *is* reliable. This is important to every Christian: after all, almost everything we known about Jesus comes from the New Testament. But it is important also because some people have claimed that the text of the Bible is *not* reliable, that it has been corrupted and changed. What we can say with confidence is that there is *no* evidence to support such charges. If Muslim teachers are to go on denying the crucifixion of Christ, or persist in explaining discrepancies between what is in the Qur'an and what is in the Old Testament or New Testament by accusing Jews and Christians of corrupting the Scriptures, or at least of allowing them to be corrupted, then they really must produce some evidence of this corruption. So far all that has been offered is the so-called *Gospel of Barnabas*, which was written in Italian or Spanish in the fifteenth or sixteenth century AD.

Perhaps one more point should be added to this consideration of the Bible. It is a book of history, and it is an inspired book, with all that that entails. But most of us know the Bible only as a *translated* book. It was originally written in Hebrew, in Aramaic (a language related to Hebrew) and in Greek. But although Greek is still spoken today it is a very different form of Greek from what was spoken in Jesus' day. And although Hebrew has been revived and established as the language of the State of Israel, that, too, is very different from Old Testament Hebrew. The customs of those days were very different from today's customs, so that it is little wonder that the translators of the Bible are not always sure how best to translate some words and sentences.

Fortunately we have scholars,

both Jews and Christians, studying the Bible, and archaeologists excavating sites named in the Bible, so that every day fresh light is being shed on the world of Bible times. As new translations of the Bible are made, so we find it more and more easy to understand the Bible's message.

It's also well worth remembering that there are many scholars, who are *not* Jews and *not* Christians, who are engaged in the study of the Bible and of the ancient manuscripts, and investigating the sites of towns and cities mentioned in the Bible. These are people who are just scholars, always ready to test and check the findings of other scholars. Therefore, with confidence, we may look on the labours of the scholars, and the results in terms of new translations of the Bible, with real thankfulness, assured that out of it all is coming honest work, a work of integrity, the authoritative and trustworthy Word of God.

The contents of the Bible

The Bible is really a library in itself, and the newcomer to the Bible may well find it very difficult to find his or her way around its pages, and even more difficult to decide just how to set about reading it.

One obvious way of getting into the Bible is by reading through the histories in order. The outline at the beginning of this chapter could well be used for that. There are many ways of reading through the Bible systematically, for example, the schemes prepared by the Scripture Union.

It is useful, however, to have a summary of the contents of the Bible. First of all the Old Testament. The Jews divide this into

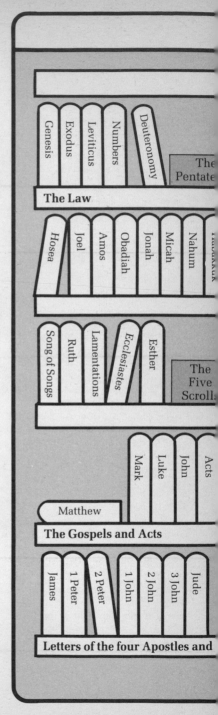

Genesis · Exodus · Leviticus · Numbers · Deuteronomy — **The Law** — The Pentate[uch]

Hosea · Joel · Amos · Obadiah · Jonah · Micah · Nahum · [Habakkuk]

Song of Songs · Ruth · Lamentations · Ecclesiastes · Esther — The Five Scroll[s]

Matthew · Mark · Luke · John · Acts — **The Gospels and Acts**

James · 1 Peter · 2 Peter · 1 John · 2 John · 3 John · Jude — **Letters of the four Apostles and**

mary of the contents of the Bible

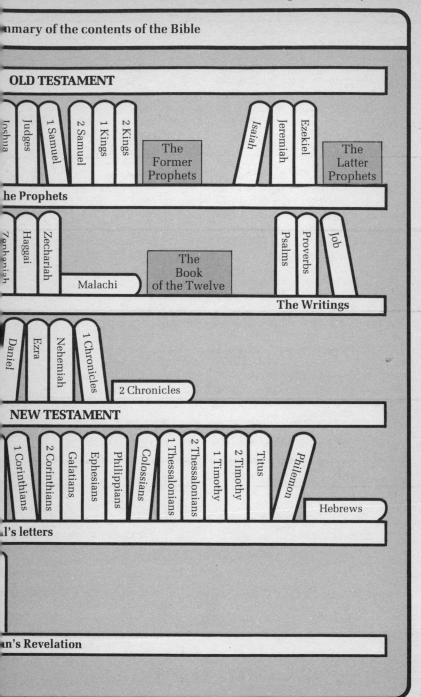

OLD TESTAMENT

Joshua · Judges · 1 Samuel · 2 Samuel · 1 Kings · 2 Kings

The Former Prophets

Isaiah · Jeremiah · Ezekiel

The Latter Prophets

he Prophets

Zephaniah · Haggai · Zechariah · Malachi

The Book of the Twelve

Psalms · Proverbs · Job

The Writings

Daniel · Ezra · Nehemiah · 1 Chronicles · 2 Chronicles

NEW TESTAMENT

1 Corinthians · 2 Corinthians · Galatians · Ephesians · Philippians · Colossians · 1 Thessalonians · 2 Thessalonians · 1 Timothy · 2 Timothy · Titus · Philemon · Hebrews

l's letters

n's Revelation

three main sections: the Law, the Prophets and the Writings. The first part, the Law, includes just five books (the 'Pentateuch'), Genesis, Exodus, Leviticus, Numbers and Deuteronomy. The first two of these are mainly history, and the other three are mainly instructional. The Prophets are divided into two groups, the Former Prophets and the Latter Prophets. The Former Prophets are mainly historical: Joshua, Judges, Samuel, Kings. The Latter Prophets are Isaiah, Jeremiah and Ezekiel, plus what is called the Book of the Twelve, Hosea, Joel, Amos, Obadiah, Jonah, Micah, Nahum, Habakkuk, Zephaniah, Haggai, Zechariah and Malachi. The Writings take in the rest of the books in three groups: Psalms, Proverbs and Job, all three poetic; the five Scrolls, the Song of Solomon, Ruth, Lamentations, Ecclesiastes and Esther; and finally another group of three, Daniel, Ezra-Nehemiah and Chronicles. Of course there are two books each to Samuel, Kings and Chronicles.

The books of the New Testament can also be divided into three groups. Like the Old Testament, the first group contains five books, the four Gospels (Matthew, Mark, Luke and John) and the Acts of the Apostles. Acts is included because it is volume two of Luke's work. The second group consists of thirteen letters written by Paul, plus Hebrews, which some people think was also written by Paul. The third group consists of seven letters, by James, Peter, John and Jude, plus the Revelation also written by John.

How to read the Bible

The Bible is not a book to be studied by the scholars and then explained to the rest of us by the experts. It represents a library for us to read and enjoy. It is the task of Bible translators to take the original Hebrew, Greek and Aramaic writings and so express them in our languages that we *can* understand them. Thousands of

Six-week Bible-reading plan

Week 1	The Gospel according to Luke (24 chapters)
Week 2	The book of Acts (also written by Luke, chapters 1–9)
Week 3	Genesis (chapters 1–4 and 6–9)
Week 4	Genesis (chapters 12–22)
Week 5	Exodus (chapters 1–24)
Week 6	Romans (chapters 1–8)

translators all over the world give their lives to this vital work.

Of course it's true that some parts of the Bible are difficult to understand. But because it is mostly about ordinary people, what they said, did, thought, and how God spoke to them through his special messengers who, also, were usually rather ordinary people, the Bible really isn't all that difficult to read and to understand. And, as one reader of the Bible once commented: 'It's not the bits of the Bible that I don't understand that bother me: it's the bits that I *do* understand'!

So . . . read it for yourself. Here's a suggestion for making a start. I believe in the value of reading the Bible in large chunks, not just a few verses. So here's a six-week programme of reading which will require about fifteen minutes each morning, and another fifteen minutes each evening. Find a quiet place, read carefully and let God speak to you out of it.

The Bible has a remarkable power of its own. That's not surprising: Christians refer to it as 'The Word of God'. So it isn't too astonishing to discover that, again and again, people who have not been persuaded by Christian preachers and writers have turned instead to the Bible . . . and have made the discovery: that's right . . . it's all true! J. B. Phillips, who made a striking translation of the New Testament, said that when he was doing his translation work, repeatedly he 'felt rather like an electrician re-wiring an ancient house without being able to "turn the mains off" '. Its particular power is the power to introduce us to Jesus.

8
Belonging together

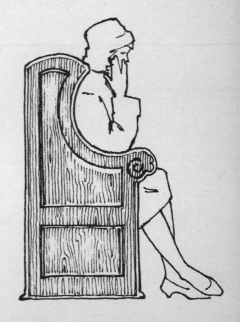

That word 'church'. To many people in the western world it means:

- wooden and uncomfortable pews
- long, tedious and irrelevant sermons
- a strange language of 'thee's, thou's and 'thus'es.

The early church *was* very different. For one thing there were no special buildings where Christians met. They met in the homes of the better-off Christians (because their homes would be bigger and so able to take the large numbers of people who wanted to come). There was a church in Philemon's home (see Philemon verse 2) and another in the home of a couple called Aquila and Priscilla (see Romans 16:3–5).

In fact in the New Testament the word 'church' never means a bricks-and-mortar building.

The word refers to the Christians who met together to worship God.

The whole notion of 'church' points to a very important aspect of Christianity: Christians are not meant to go it alone. Becoming a Christian means becoming part of a world-wide family, whose head is God. This family is now so large that it's no longer possible for the whole family to meet together, so they meet in small local 'families' or churches.

This principle of 'togetherness' is important for all of us. Right at the beginning God had made clear a principle that is fundamental to everyone: it is not good to be alone (see Genesis 2:18).

Marriage is given to us not merely so that we could have children. Sex without marriage could take care of that. Marriage is there for the lifelong comfort and help that man and wife can expect from each other. The church is another gift of God which ensures that we do enjoy family life even if we aren't married, or even if husband or wife is abandoned because of becoming a Christian. Christianity is more than conversion: it is also incorporation into the world-wide family of God, and into a local family of Christians, the church.

We need the friendship and help of other Christians, partly because it is unhealthy and unnatural for us to be loners. Naturally we should be gregarious, enjoying being with people. But there is another reason why we need the church: we need the help and encouragement of other Christians. We sometimes divide the world-wide church into two parts, the 'church militant' and the 'church triumphant'. Those two labels are well chosen. The church *militant* is the church on earth; the church triumphant is the church at home in heaven. The church here is *militant* because it is engaged in spiritual battle. The Christian life is not merely a Sunday afternoon stroll by the river, but a battle.

This battle is a spiritual one. We are not at war with *people*. There is spiritual opposition, however, that we are certain to encounter. Paul explains it all very clearly:

> *Finally, be strong in the Lord and in his mighty power. Put on the full armour of God so that you can take your stand against the devil's schemes. For our struggle is not against flesh and blood, but against the rulers, against the authorities, against the powers of this dark world and against the spiritual forces of evil in the heavenly realms* (Ephesians 6:10–12).

We need the help and encouragement of other Christians, of our church, in this spiritual conflict.

The two kingdoms

In chapter two we looked at what Jesus had said about the kingdom of God. Paul's words to the Ephesian Christians is a reminder that Christianity recognizes an evil power that is opposed to that kingdom. This again is one of the fundamental beliefs of Christianity, part of the world-view that the Bible presents to us. In addition to the material world which we can see, feel, hear and smell, there is another world. Both worlds are entirely real, entwined and linked together in myriad ways. There is the human conscience, for example, which, however twisted it may become, will still from time to time make us uneasy with its insistence: 'That's wrong.' There are human emotions, which aren't *material*: love, hate, anger, joy, awe, hope, despair. These, too, point beyond the material things by which we are surrounded to things that can't be touched, measured, or weighed, but are still real.

So we aren't materialists. We do know something of the non-material world. But that world, like this material world, is a divided one. The evil that we can so easily see in this world is there in the non-material world, too. Sin is at work in both. In fact we are to recognize two warring kingdoms:

- the kingdom of this world
- the kingdom of God.

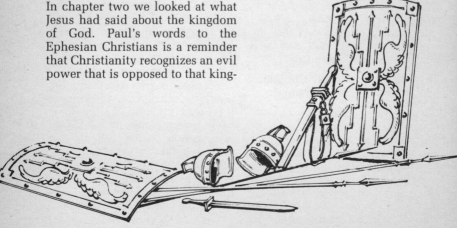

The kingdom of this world is a kingdom dominated by the ideas, standards, morals, hates, fears and desires of people who have never experienced the new start, the new birth, which Christianity offers.

It has a leader, Satan. It has its messengers, evil spirits. The reality of the conflict between these two worlds is probably best seen in the account given by Luke of the temptation of Jesus (see Luke 4:1–13).

Jesus was full of the Holy Spirit, and was led by him and yet he was tempted by Satan. It is a comfort to learn from this that there is nothing wrong with being *tempted*. That's no sin! Jesus was not tempted, however, by some vague 'impulse', whatever that might mean. He was tempted by a person, Satan. Two common words used to name him are *Satan*, from Hebrew, and *the devil*, from the Greek *diabolos*. These words mean 'Adversary'. In the desert, Jesus met the Adversary, Satan, who was determined to make Jesus sin, to do something, anything, that was not part of God's will for him. That conflict between Jesus and the devil is a good, clear illustration of the kind of conflict in which Christians will always be engaged. We need the church, the help and encouragement of other Christians, if we are to win as Jesus did.

The church is the sphere within which the rule of God is recognized. It is the gathering of the people of God to do the will of God. In the church God rules! But precisely because we are in the church we shall find ourselves battling with temptation, much as Jesus did. So often it is the help and encouragement of other Christians that will enable us to hold on, to remain faithful, to look to God for the courage and strength that

we need if we are to live the way God wants us to. We need the church.

The divided church

The churches are divided. There are hundreds of different groups, divided on all kinds of issues, some important, some unimportant. Sometimes the divisions are much more a matter of personalities than of doctrines. However there *is* only one 'holy, catholic,* church'. It is the world-wide family of God consisting of all those who are true followers of Jesus. So how are we to explain the divisions?

It is possible to be very positive about the denominations because they do present *variety*. Because there are Methodist, Baptist and Anglican churches near my home I can choose which of them to attend. Actually, if I ask myself *why* I attend the church I now go to, the answer will most probably not be a theological answer. It's more likely to be sociological: I like the people who go there, the kind of music they have, the preacher, it's near my home, my parents used to go there, and so on. My choice often seems to have little to do with theology.

In fact most of us don't know much about the beliefs of other churches. Some years ago I wrote an article in the British Weekly in which I suggested that most Baptists don't know why they aren't Methodists, and most Methodists don't know why they aren't Anglicans, and most Plymouth Brethren don't know why they aren't Baptists. The following week there was an irate letter from a certain man.

*See the note on this important word at the top of the diagram on the next page.

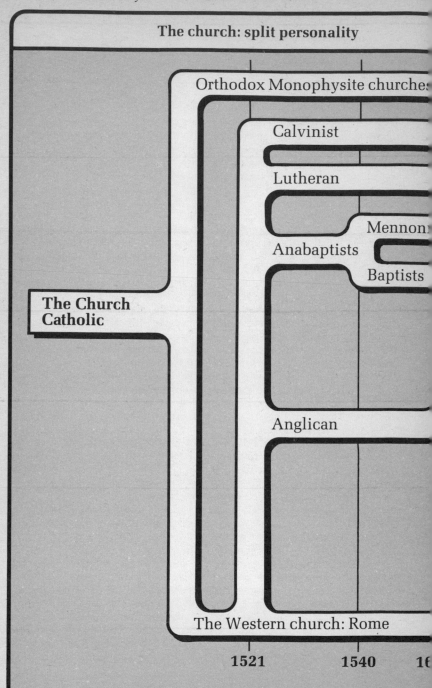

The church: split personality

Orthodox Monophysite churches

Calvinist

Lutheran

Mennon

Anabaptists

Baptists

**The Church
Catholic**

Anglican

The Western church: Rome

1521   1540   16

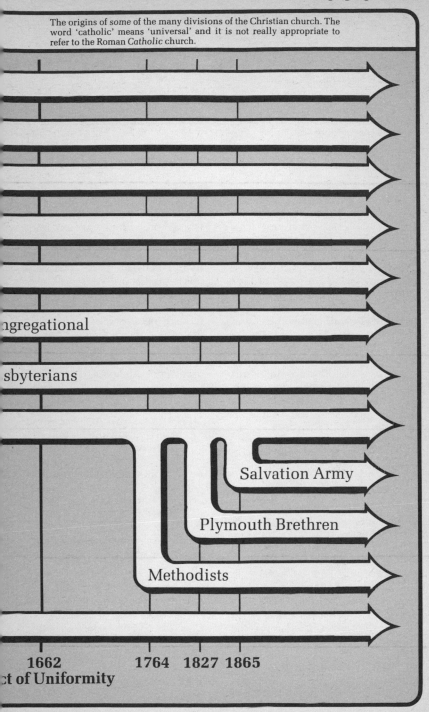

The origins of some of the many divisions of the Christian church. The word 'catholic' means 'universal' and it is not really appropriate to refer to the Roman *Catholic* church.

ngregational

sbyterians

Salvation Army

Plymouth Brethren

Methodists

1662   **1764** **1827 1865**
t of Uniformity

He most certainly *did* know why he was Brethren, and not Baptist. He proceeded to list (I think) ten reasons. In every one of those ten he showed that he misunderstood what Baptists believe and practise!

I'm really not as concerned as some people are about these denominational differences. They tend *now*, whatever they may have been originally, to be an expression of cultural differences. Some have a kind of jazz-band culture, and others more of a symphony concert culture. It does make it possible for us all to find a church where we will feel at ease; where we can worship God and feel comfortable about it. Trouble comes when the jazz-band people insist that everyone ought to have a jazz-band, or when the symphony concert church up the road starts preaching that all jazz-bands are of the devil.

Of course there *are* doctrinal differences, but if we were to be honest we would have to admit that very few Christians understand them. There has to be a balance between assuming that doctrine doesn't matter at all (which is rather like suggesting that when you are on a voyage you can ignore the compass) and insisting that everyone must believe exactly what I believe (which is rather like saying that we should all have identical compasses). C. S. Lewis helps here. In his *Screwtape letters*[1] we have a collection of letters from Screwtape, a rather superior sort of devil, to Wormwood, a rather lowly tempter. Screwtape is advising Wormwood on how to deal with this question of a Christian joining a church:

I think I warned you before that if your patient can't be kept out of the church, he ought at least to

be violently attached to some party within it. I don't mean on really doctrinal issues; about those, the more lukewarm he is the better. And it isn't the doctrines on which we chiefly depend for producing malice. The real fun is working up hatred between those who *say* 'mass' and those who *say* 'holy communion' when neither party could possibly state the difference between, say, Hooker's doctrine and Thomas Aquinas', in any form which would hold water for five minutes (*Screwtape Letters*, chapter XVI).

On the other side, sadly, one must respond negatively to the divisions in the church, because so often they are not merely due to honestly held differences of opinion, in which each respects the view of the other, but evidences of pride, of bitterness, of grudges nursed, nurtured and aired over many years. Divisions like these are contrary to the will of God. Christians can only be ashamed of them. Jesus himself *prayed* for the unity of his church:

'*My prayer is not for them* [the apostles] *alone. I pray also for those who will believe in me through their message, that all of them may be one, Father, just as you are in me and I am in you. May they also be in us so that the world may believe that you have sent me. I have given them the glory that you gave me, that they may be one as we are one: I in them and you in me. May they be brought to complete unity to let the world know that you sent me and have loved them even as you have loved me'* (John 17:20–23).

This prayer of Jesus is interesting because it does indicate the kind of unity that he has in mind for his church. It is like the unity that there is between Father and Son, which is tremendously significant. This does not suggest *integration*, as though the Son stopped being the Son and lost his identity. The unity between Father and Son is one of will, purpose and love. That, it seems to me, is the kind of unity we should look for in the churches. This is just one of the reasons why I feel that the World Council of Churches has got it wrong. The Council has done its best to promote schemes of *integration*, in which real differences are submerged and churches lose their identity. Rather we need to look for unity of purpose, while being prepared to accept real differences in the way we do things. Ephesians 4:2–16 sums it up so clearly.

Ephesians 4:2–7, 11–16

Be completely humble and gentle; be patient, bearing with one another in love. Make every effort to keep the unity of the Spirit through the bond of peace. There is one body and one Spirit – just as you were called to one hope when you were called – one Lord, one faith, one baptism; one God and Father of all, who is over all and through all and in all.

But to each one of us grace has been given as Christ apportioned it … It was he who gave some to be apostles, some to be prophets, some to be evangelists and some to be pastors and teachers, to prepare God's people for works of service, so that the body of Christ may be built up until we all reach unity in the faith and in the knowledge of the Son of God, and become mature, attaining to the whole measure of the fulness of Christ.

Then we will no longer be infants, tossed back and forth by the waves, and blown here and there by every wind of teaching and by the cunning and craftiness of men in their deceitful scheming. Instead, speaking the truth in love, we will in all things grow up into him who is the Head, that is, Christ. From him the whole body, joined and held together by every supporting ligament, grows and builds itself up in love, as each part does its work.

The purpose of the Church

What is the church *for*? The church is there primarily for three things: community, worship and witness. The first of this trio, *community*, has two aspects to it: the church's relationship to other Christians, and its relationship to the non-Christian world.

Fellowship

So far as the church's relationship towards Christian people is concerned, the appropriate word to describe it is *fellowship* (the New Testament word is *koinōnia*). It is the obvious characteristic of the church as a family. This 'family' idea often astonishes non-

Christians. I served in the Royal Air Force for two years and was sent off to the north of England. The first Sunday that I was permitted to leave camp I set off to find a church, and got back to camp late that night. And then the questions began. Where had I been all day? 'I went to church.' That was clear enough, but where did I have my dinner? 'Oh, some people at the church took me home with them to dinner.' Did I know them before? 'No, I'd never set eyes on them previously.' Well, what about tea? 'I had tea with another family ... and supper with another family ... no, I didn't know them, previously, either.' The other men were frankly bewildered. They simply had no

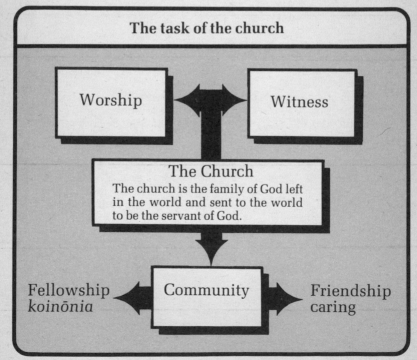

The task of the church

Worship

Witness

The Church

The church is the family of God left in the world and sent to the world to be the servant of God.

Community

Fellowship
koinōnia

Friendship
caring

TEAR Fund at work in Kenya

experience of a family like that ... the family of the church. Now I *know* that not all churches are like that. But many are, and all should be.

This idea of *koinōnia* means 'sharing', allowing others, welcoming others, to share in the good things we have. The idea is clearly demonstrated in the beginnings of the church in Jerusalem.

On the Day of Pentecost Peter preached, and something like three thousand people responded to that preaching. This is what the Bible says about them:

They devoted themselves to the apostles' teaching, and to the fellowship, to the breaking of bread and to prayer ... All the believers were together and had everything in common ... They broke bread in their homes and ate together with glad and sincere hearts, praising God and enjoying the favour of all the people (Acts 2:42–47).

There is a similar kind of relationship between the church and the non-Christian community. It can't really be called *koinōnia* because very often there's very little in common between the two. What is offered by the church might be labelled *friendship*, or caring. The church does not treat its non-Christian neighbours as enemies. It is always there trying to help. Paul wrote to the Christians in Galatia:

Therefore, as we have opportunity, let us do good to all people, especially to those who belong to the family of believers (Galatians 6:10).

Let us do good to *all* people. At the local level this means that the church should be offering unconditional love, even and especially to those who are left out by the rest of society. That explains the large number of 'odd' people we often find in the churches. They find in the church the kindness that simply isn't offered to them by anyone else. At the international level this idea of doing good to everyone explains the existence of organizations such as TEAR Fund (**T**he **E**vangelical **A**lliance **R**elief Fund) which takes the love and concern of the church out to parts of the world that can't be reached by the local church.

Worship

The second primary activity of the church is *worship*. Of *course* it is possible to worship God on your own, but it is a marvellous thing to be able to join together with other Christians, maybe hundreds of them, to worship God as a family. Jesus taught his followers only one prayer, and that began 'Our *Father*' (Matthew 6:9–13). You can't really pray that prayer on your own. It's a family prayer. Christians are expected to meet together, regularly, to have fellowship and to worship God. Jesus quite deliberately took a well-known saying of the Jewish Rabbis of his day and changed it slightly. *They* used to say, 'Where two or three are gathered to study the Torah (the Law of Moses), there God is with them'. Jesus said, '*Where two or three come together in my name, there am I with them*' (Matthew 18:20). Worship is a recognition of this presence among us. In fact one useful definition of worship is 'the proper response to an awareness of the presence of God'. You can see it in Moses, called up to Mount Sinai and given a remarkable vision of God ... '*Then the Lord came down in the cloud and stood there with him ... Moses bowed to the ground at once and worshipped*' (Exodus 34:5,8).

Witness

So the church is for *community* and for *worship*. It is also there for *witness*. Christians are people who have encountered God through Jesus, and who have admitted their sinfulness, and repenting find forgiveness through the death of Jesus. Christians are people who have received the Holy Spirit and so have power to live quite differently. But the enormous question asked by the non-Christian world is: does it work? The Christian is the witness who can say, 'It *does* work, because it works for me.' It isn't always necessary to explain *how* Christianity works, but it surely is necessary for us to show in our lives that it *does* work. Take as an illustration the story, in John chapter 9, about an unnamed man who was blind, but whose sight was restored by Jesus. The Pharisees interrogated him about this miracle. They asked him *how* it was done and the man told them (verse 15). But then they wanted to get involved in the theology of the miracle: 'We know that this man is a sinner' (verse 24). The man couldn't comment on that. He was no theologian. He stuck firmly to what he knew:

> '*Whether he is a sinner or not, I don't know. One thing I do know: I was blind but now I see!*' (verse 25).

Maybe we have not experienced a miracle of healing quite like that, but we are expected to witness like that: to tell others what God has done for us.

We may not have to do it by talking about it. Our lives should show the love of God. Christians should be excellent neighbours to have, excellent employers and employees, excellent wives, husbands, sons, daughters. Christianity is intended to produce good people, and we should be able to see God at work producing them. But very quickly the time will come when someone will ask us about our faith. I remember, when I was living in Addis Ababa, that a man who worked at the United Nations there was taken seriously ill with schizophrenia. His wife was desperate: she knew nobody. We did our best to help. We took her meals to the hospital where her husband was so ill. We took turns watching him while she went off to get some rest. It went on like this for about a month, and I suppose that all through that time she was watching us, wondering about our motives. We were standing on the balcony outside her husband's ward and suddenly she turned to me and asked,

'Peter, how can I become a Christian?'

We need to be able to answer a question like that. The church should have that as one of its tasks: preparing Christians to be witnesses.

There's overseas witness, too. The church is there to be obedient to Jesus' own command to *go and make disciples of all nations* (Matthew 28:19), and to receive from the churches of the world God's messengers, who are being called to witness to us. For witness is not just me telling others what God has done in my life: it also means listening to what God has done in the lives of other people. The marvellous fact is that God is at work in his church all over the world, and it can be thrilling to listen to the voices of the church in Africa, South America and India.

A selection of church buildings in South America and Africa

9
The goal of history

circles: then life is hopeless. But the Bible promises that history has a climax. The world does not go out with a whimper, nor even with a bang. It is ended when the purpose for which God made it has been satisfied.

The basic questions with which we started this book produce answers which make clear the world-views of the world's religions. The acceptance of a religion always means the acceptance of a particular world-view, a particular way of understanding and explaining life. The world-views that emerge are many and they are all different. The Christian world-view may be set out concisely:

If history goes on for ever: that is boring. If history simply fades away as man fades away: that is anticlimax. If history goes round in

The Christian world view

1 The world is not a mere cosmic accident. God created it, and created it purposefully.

2 Man is not merely the chance product of evolution, another cosmic accident. He is created by God. He is different from all other forms of life because he shares in the nature of God. He was created in the image of God (see Genesis 1:26). God has planted the idea of eternity into man's mind (see Ecclesiastes 3:11) so that he *knows* that there is something beyond this world.

3 Life is unsatisfactory. But it is unsatisfactory not merely as a result of our ignorance, but as a result of our sin. We try in vain to live life without God.

4 The unsatisfactoriness of life will never be solved by human wisdom, by human governments,

by international organizations, however well-meaning they may be. The only answer is to reconcile man with God, because only man who is reconciled to God can also be reconciled to man.

5 Man can be reconciled to God only through Christ. The central act of human history was the death of Christ on the cross on behalf of sinners. In this act we do not find a man making a generous action as an example to the rest of us, but we find God stepping into the world and carrying away its sin.

6 Reconciliation with God is accompanied by the gift of the Holy Spirit, who alone can give us new life, new strength, enabling us on the one hand to defeat sin and on the other hand to live positively good lives.

7 God has his people throughout

the world and they are his servants. Through the church and through the churches their task is to witness to the world, to tell the world of what God's answer is to the world's cry for help. The church is to represent God, to show his compassion through acts of love, through giving, through self-sacrifice.

8 But there is also to be a message of warning, a warning that the kingdom of God is a reality, and that while we are now called to enter that kingdom, refusal to enter it, or rejection of the invitation, leaves us to bear the consequences of our sin ourselves.

9 The world will not merely run down as energy becomes less and less available, as scientists have suggested, nor will it end in some massive catastrophe brought about by nuclear holocaust, as some sociologists have suggested, but by a definite act of God.

10 The ending of the world's history will usher in judgment, and it is this judgment that will balance the books, establish God's justice, make it clear that, contrary to all experience hitherto, life *is* fair because life is more than *this* life.

The idea of judgment

The judgment at the end of the world is an event when things will be seen as they really are and were. At present we cannot see things as they are: we see only the externals. We see *what* is being done, but we don't understand *why* it is being done. This is true of good actions as well as of bad actions. We may see a Christian writing a cheque for a large sum of money to a missionary society, but we don't know *why* he is writing it. Is he really concerned about the good that the missionaries might do? Is he concerned rather to ensure that people know how generously he gives and so earn their applause? Is he trying to make up for some sin that he has committed, trying to buy God off? We don't know. A poor man steals a loaf of bread. Is it just that he has got accustomed to stealing, is it that he finds stealing exciting, or is it that his family has nothing to eat? We don't know.

This is all part of the general unfairness of life. We know about some good actions, some bad actions, but we don't really know much about the reasons for those actions. There are many good actions and many wrong actions of which we know nothing at all. So of course we can't balance the account. Of course life seems unfair. Our situation is rather like that of an accountant who is trying to produce an accurate statement of a company's activities but is allowed to see only one cheque book out of every ten, one ledger out of every six, one bank statement out of every twenty, and so on. Without the facts the task simply can't be carried out; not properly, at any rate.

The Bible is shot through with references to a day of judgment. In his letter to the church at Rome, Paul made reference to the complexity of judgment, bearing in mind the difference between all that the Jews had by way of God's revelation, and the little that the non-Jewish world had. But still he insisted that one day all would be made clear:

> This will take place on the day when God will judge men's secrets through Jesus Christ, as my gospel declares (Romans 2:16).

It is significant that Paul relates this day of judgment to the person of Jesus, 'through Jesus Christ'. This is an indication that the last judgment is essentially not a mere adding up of good deeds and bad deeds to see which outweighs the other. Instead it is a judgment which relates to our reponse to Jesus. Jesus was crucified for us, and died for us. What has been our response to that sacrifice:

> But now he has appeared once for all at the end of the ages to do away with sin by the sacrifice of himself. Just as man is destined to die once, and after that to face judgment, so Christ was sacrificed once to take away the sins of many people; and he will appear a second time, not to bear sin, but to bring salvation to those who are waiting for him (Hebrews 9:26–28).

Now the outline of the Bible's teaching on the day of judgment is beginning to appear. Jesus is to come again, 'he will appear a second time'. Actually this fact was announced to Jesus' first followers immediately after his ascension. They were still standing, staring upwards to the cloud which had hidden him from their sight, when they were told:

> 'This same Jesus, who has been taken from you into heaven, will come back in the same way you have seen him go into heaven' (Acts 1:11).

The return of Jesus is vividly pictured in 1 Thessalonians 4:16:

> For the Lord himself will come down from heaven, with a loud command, with the voice of the archangel and with the trumpet call of God.

This verse is itself just part of a mosaic which finally adds up to an unforgettable picture of the end time. Paul affirms:

> . . . we will all be changed – in a flash, in the twinkling of an eye, at the last trumpet. For the trumpet will sound, the dead will be raised imperishable, and we will be changed (1 Corinthians 15:51–52).

Jesus himself added a striking illustration of the suddenness of the end:

> Two men will be in the field; one will be taken and the other left. Two women will be grinding with a hand mill; one will be taken and the other left (Matthew 24:40–41).

We are left to imagine the astonishment of the man left alone in the

field, the woman whose friend has simply vanished . . .

So often the critics have smiled at what they consider the naïve ideas of Christianity concerning the end time. *That* isn't unexpected either. Peter contributes to the mosaic:

> They will say, 'Where is this "coming" he promised? Ever since our fathers died everything goes on as it has since the beginning of creation' (2 Peter 3:4).

And as Peter comments drily, things haven't gone on smoothly from generation to generation. There is the flood of Genesis 6 to warn us that God *may* intervene in our affairs, drastically. And in any case, time is very different for God, in his eternal 'now', from what it is for us with our pathetically limited sixty or seventy years. Isaiah adds his comment on prophecy:

> I foretold the former things long ago,
>   my mouth announced them and I made them known;
>   then suddenly I acted, and they came to pass
> (Isaiah 48:3).

There is to be a Day of Judgment. But notice that in all this talk about the end of time and judgment there is always a careful distinction made between what the *Christian* will experience at the end time, and what *the rest* will experience.

The appearance of Christ at the end of the world is 'to bring salvation to those who are waiting for him' (Hewbrews 9:28). That is clear enough, but what is the significance of his coming for those who are *not* waiting for him? The answer there is judgment.

Here we *are* faced with a problem. Not everyone has heard the good news about Jesus. It is still true that for the vast majority of

people their religion is largely determined for them by the accident of birth. The person who is born in India is likely to be a Hindu, the person born in Saudi Arabia is likely to be a Muslim, and the person who is born in America is likely to be a Christian. So how are they to be judged? Paul, preaching in Athens, indicates an answer:

> For he has set a day when he will judge the world with justice by the man he has appointed. He has given proof of this to all men by raising him from the dead (Acts 17:31).

Once again there is confirmation that judgment is to be by Jesus, the one who was raised from the dead, but this judgment is to be *just*. The point about justice is neatly brought out by Abraham over the question of God's determination to judge and destroy the city of Sodom. Abraham raises the question of the possibility that in that city there might be some good people:

> 'What if there are fifty righteous people in the city? Will you really sweep it away and not spare the place for the sake of the fifty righteous people in it? Far be it from you to do such a thing – to kill the righteous with the wicked, treating the righteous and the wicked alike. Far be it from you! Will not the Judge of all the earth do right?' (Genesis 18: 24–25).

It is interesting to note that in his reply God does not simply respond that Abraham doesn't know what he's talking about, and that God, because he is God, can do as he likes. He accepts Abraham's point. We do have an idea of *justice* and God assures Abraham that he *will* act justly.

One further comment should be made on this point. The problem of what God will do about those who have not heard the good news about Jesus is not my problem, nor is it yours. If you've read this far, then you *have* heard about Jesus. We can go further, and say that God's response to our questioning on behalf of those who have not heard the good news is to tell us to go and share the good news with them. What we can be sure of is that at the last judgment God will judge the world *justly* and he will do it through Jesus.

This brings us firmly back to where the book started, the idea of religion as providing answers to the basic human questions. Christianity does provide clear answers to these questions, but they are not the same answers as the answers offered by other religions. All religions seem to agree on just this one point: life is unsatisfactory. Good is not rewarded, evil is not punished. God's response, in simple terms, is: 'I have dealt with your sins through the sacrifice of my Son on the cross. I have dealt with your powerlessness through my Spirit, given to those who will follow my Son. This is what you need in order to make sense of the world.' And if we reject it?

If we deliberately keep on sinning after we have received the knowledge of the truth, no sacrifice for sins is left, but only a fearful expectation of judgment (Hebrews 10:26).

Revelation 20:11–12, 15 — 21:4

Then I saw a great white throne and him who was seated on it. Earth and sky fled from his presence, and there was no place for them. And I saw the dead, great and small, standing before the throne, and books were opened. Another book was opened, which is the book of life. The dead were judged according to what they had done as recorded in the books . . .

If anyone's name was not found written in the book of life, he was thrown into the lake of fire.

Then I saw a new heaven and a new earth, for the first heaven and the first earth had passed away, and there was no longer any sea. I saw the Holy City, the new Jerusalem, coming down out of heaven from God, prepared as a bride beautifully dressed for her husband. And I heard a loud voice from the throne saying, 'Now

the dwelling of God is with men, and he will live with them. They will be his people, and God himself will be with them and be their God. He will wipe every tear from their eyes. There will be no more death or mourning or crying or pain, for the old order of things has passed away.'

The Lamb's Book of Life

In the dramatic vision of the judgment passed on to us by John in Revelation 20:11 – 21:4 there is reference to books, and to '*the book of life*' (20:12). This particular book is mentioned again in Revelation 21:27, but this time with a striking addition: it is the *Lamb's* book of life.

This clue sends us back to the first chapter of John's Gospel. John the Baptist catches his first glimpse of Jesus, points to him and calls out to the crowd around him:

'*Look, the Lamb of God, who takes away the sin of the world!*' (John 1:29).

The Lamb's book of life. The Lamb of God. Why '*Lamb*'?

There are three clear Old Testament indications of the answer:

1 Jesus is being compared to the lamb that was killed by the Israelites in Egypt at the first Passover. They were then slaves in Egypt, but the Passover signalled God's determination to set them free. We have in Exodus chapter 12 an account of the death of the eldest son in every Egyptian home, and of the safety of the eldest sons in the homes of the Israelites through the symbolic killing of a lamb, the blood of which was then splashed on the door frame. The connection of *that* event with the death of Jesus is made certain by the fact that Jesus was crucified at the Passover feast. So Jesus is to be seen as in some sense a fulfilment of the Passover sacrifice of a lamb.

2 Jesus is being likened to the Servant of the Lord in Isaiah 53:7, '*he was led like a lamb to the*

slaughter.' We looked briefly at the Servant songs in chapter three, but again we must ask: 'Who is the Servant of the Lord?'

In some passages it is quite clear that Israel is the servant (Isaiah 44:1), but then Isaiah 49:6 talks about the servant *restoring* Israel, so the two can't be the same in that passage. In Isaiah chapter 53 the servant is quite clearly an *individual* who can grow up, be despised, can suffer, be afflicted, killed, buried, and yet see afterwards that it was all worth while. Jesus is to be seen as a fulfilment of Isaiah's prophecy of a Servant who would suffer and through that suffering would bring not only Israel but the rest of the nations back to God (Isaiah 49:6).

3 In Leviticus chapter 16 there is reference to a ceremony in which, symbolically, the sins of the people were carried away into the desert by a goat. This particular ceremony formed just part of the larger ceremony connected with the most important day in the Hebrew calendar, the Day of Atonement. It was on this day that the involuntary, unintentional sins of the people during the year past were in symbol dealt with. Jesus is being seen as the Lamb of God who carries away the sins of the people. This equation is confirmed by the remarkable event that occurred immediately following the death of Christ on the cross:

> The curtain of the temple was torn in two from top to bottom (Mark 15:38).

Now that curtain had marked the division between the two central parts of the Temple, the Holy Place and the Most Holy Place. The High Priest alone was allowed into the Most Holy Place, and even he went in there just once each year, on the Day of Atonement. So the tearing away of the curtain directs our attention to a link between the Day of Atonement and the crucifixion of Christ, to the fact that it is Jesus who deals with our sin, and to the fact that he fulfilled the imagery of the goat which 'took away' into the desert the sins of the people.

Each of these Old Testament pictures provides some part of the explanation of the phrase 'The Lamb of God', and each picture is in some sense deficient. Putting together the three pictures strikingly explains John's phrase, although obviously this rather protracted explanation given here would not have been necessary to the crowd listening to John the Baptist. Jesus is the Lamb of Passover, the substitute who frees us not from slavery in Egypt but from our captivity to sin. Jesus is the Servant of the Lord, the Lamb who uncomplainingly suffers, crushed for our iniquities. Jesus is the Lamb of God who carries away the sins of the world.

Now we can return to the Lamb's book of life. The books to which John refers are the records of our lives. The evidence that makes the judgment of the Judge so obviously just is all there in the books. There can be no question of a clever lawyer confusing the Judge with rhetoric, no question of a large bribe to suppress part of the evidence. The books are open.

But if judgment were to proceed from those books alone there could be no hope for anyone. It is impossible to imagine anyone, anywhere, who could face an investigation in which every half-truth, every act of impatience, every unkindness, even every omission were indelibly, unfailingly recorded. It is simply impossible to imagine that the pathetic collection of really good deeds that I could muster in my defence could ever outweigh the mass of wrong acts of which I am undoubtedly guilty. Thank God there is another book, the 'Lamb's book of life'. It is Jesus' book, in which is recorded the names of those who through the centuries have abandoned their own attempt to establish their own goodness, and instead have fled to God for refuge. These are the names of those who have admitted that they couldn't do what they knew to be right, nor evade what they knew to be wrong. They accepted Jesus' offer to bear away their sin.

It is their names that appear in the book; it is they who enter heaven.

I recall the perplexity of a man who simply didn't understand the heart of Christianity, which is complete and free forgiveness through the sheer grace of God. A man was dying. He had lived an appalling life. Yet, on the very brink of death, he repented, received Christ, and was assured of salvation. The man watching this extraordinary transformation queried tremblingly:

'Can a death-bed repentance atone for a lifetime of wickedness?'
'No,' he was told, 'but Calvary can.'

'Calvary' was the Latin name for the place where Jesus died. Here, urged on by Jewish authorities, Roman soldiers put Jesus to death on a cross, on which was nailed a paradoxical accusation in Latin, Greek and Hebrew, 'JESUS OF NAZARETH, THE KING OF THE JEWS' (John 19:19). Calvary was where God showed that he was *not* oblivious to the cry of pain from the world that he had made; where he showed his love, offered us his grace, made forgiveness and reconciliation possible, gave *his* answer to the swelling cry of the world, its '*dukkha*' cry.

Here is God's answer: Christ suffering unfairly, dying uncomplainingly, rising from death triumphantly, and offering himself unreservedly as Saviour and Lord to every one of us.

But is it true? I say with all my heart: it is!

And you?

Notes

Chapter 1

[1]John Kane, *Pluralism and Truth* (Scholars Press, 1982), p.17.

[2]C. S. Lewis, *Mere Christianity* (Fontana, 1970), p.137.

[3]L. Kolakowski, *Main Currents of Marxism* (OUP, 1982), vol. 3, pp.81–83.

Chapter 2

[2]Seyyed Hossein Nasr, *Islamic Life and Thought* (Allen and Unwin, 1981), p.19.

[2]G. B. Caird, *The Language and Imagery of the Bible* (Duckworth, 1981), p.60.

Chapter 3

[1]G. B. Caird, *The Language and Imagery of the Bible* (Duckworth, 1981), p.58.

[2]Seyyed Hossein Nasr, *Islamic Life and Thought* (Allen and Unwin, 1981), pp.209–210.

[3]M. Z. Khan, *Deliverance from the Cross* (The London Mosque, 1978), p.89.

Chapter 4

[1]Bruce Metzger, *Historical and Literary Studies* (Brill, 1968), p.11.

[1]J. N. D. Anderson, *Christianity and World Religions* (IVP, 1984), chapter 2.

Chapter 5

[1]Vincent Donovan, *Christianity Rediscovered* (SCM, 1982), p.63.

Chapter 6

[1]Vincent Donovan, *Christianity Rediscovered* (SCM, 1982), pp.85–86.

[2]C. S. Lewis, *Mere Christianity* (Fontana, 1970), p.138.

Chapter 7

[1]K. Popper, *The Open Society and Its Enemies*, **2** (Routledge, 1966), p.270.

[2]A. E. Harvey, *Jesus and the Constraints of History* (Duckworth, 1982), pp.3–4.

Chapter 8

[1]C. S. Lewis, *The Screwtape Letters* (Fount, 1982), chapter 16.

Suggested further reading

J. N. D. Anderson, *Jesus Christ: the Witness of History* (IVP, 1985).

J. N. D. Anderson, *Christianity and World Religions* (IVP, 1984).

Jo Bramwell, *Listen to the Lord* (IVP, 1983).

F. F. Bruce, *The Books and the Parchments* (Pickering & Inglis, 1972).

F. F. Bruce, *The New Testament Documents* (IVP, 1960).

Colin Chapman, *The Case for Christianity* (Lion, 1983).

Know Your Bible (IVP, 1984).

Myrtle Langley, *Religions* (Lion, 1981).

Bruce Milne, *Know the Truth* (IVP, 1982).

Frank Morison, *Who Moved the Stone?* (S.T.L., 1983)

Michael Nazir-Ali, *Islam: a Christian Perspective* (Paternoster, 1983).

John Stott, *The Bible: Book for Today* (IVP, 1982).

Acknowledgments

Picture credits: Heather Angel, 10, 63, 69 (top); Barnaby's Picture Library, 19, 42, 44, 49, 53, 64, 65, 68 (top); Camera Press, 7, 9, 21, 34, 54, 59, 68 (bottom), 81, 97 (bottom left and top right), 104; J. Allan Cash Ltd, 12, 22, 69 (bottom); Peter Cotterell, 97 (centre and bottom right); *Illustrated Bible Dictionary* (IVP, Part 3, p.1180), 20; TEAR Fund, 95.

All line illustrations are by Cliff Pyne.